dreamer.

For Dominic Dylah,
The world is yours for the taking and you have much to give to
it. You are a favored man. You are a blessed man. You are greatness.
Don't ever be afraid to dream. Even more, don't ever be afraid to
live. God's got you, and as much as you'll let me, I got you.

For Cecile Doris,
I don't know how death works, but I hope that God's giving you
special treatment up there with a view of me to boot. Véyé sa, eh.

TABLE OF CONTENTS

foreword

I have always taken comfort in the story of Joseph the Dreamer. As a dreamer myself I consider Joseph's life to be the ultimate illustration of God's promise-keeping character. It's a character that remains intact and is even amplified by the maze of hills and valleys that he allows.

At each stage of Joseph's journey there are myriad lessons for anyone cursed with a vision that seems misplaced in their reality. Having read and taught this scripture many times, I believed I had identified every lesson there is to learn. That is until I read, dreamer.

In this writing, Chadia does something masterful, as she (perhaps unknowingly) parallels her life with Joseph's. But there is more. We know how Joseph's story ends, but we find Chadia in the middle of her journey. And so, this is a testimony of faith in what is to come, not only for Chadia, but for all of us who believe that our steps are divinely ordered.

This book is for you, dreamer.

As you read, you will relate to every word, as did I. These words are light. They will illuminate the colours of your special cloak, and the darkness of your pit. They will show you people, both those who help and hurt, and enable you to discern their intentions. They will light your way from Potiphar's house to prison, and onward to your true destiny. They will remind you of the faithful God who put the dream in you. They will inspire you to keep going.

Chadia is not the first person to write about Joseph's life, nor will she be the last. But this offering may well be among the most refreshing studies you will encounter. There is profound grace, humility, humour, and honesty in these pages. Chadia weaves together a solid theological exploration and personal experiences to produce an enjoyable read for all of us.

Finally, as you turn the page to Chapter 1, I hope you appreciate the author's obedience which has brought us here. By the end of this book you too will be grateful that Chadia submitted herself as a vessel for this important creative and evangelical endeavour.

Now turn to your neighbor and say "I'm ready to turn the page."

GOLDA LEE BRUCE
Author
goldaleebruce.com

introduction

At 11:23pm GMT on April 14th, 2020, I started off a conversation with a virtual stranger. These were the words:

"I'm supremely frustrated with life.

I have numerous interests and passions and don't know which to pursue.

I have prayed.

Taken counsel.

Waited.

I'm unsatisfied with where my life is, to be honest.

I do a lot, but I don't feel like I'm financially compensated for what I give.

'Ah fed up."

At 29, I've done a few things. I've written and published 3 books under my own publishing house and even helped other Caribbean authors successfully publish their own work. I've graced stages with internationally acclaimed musicians, I've spoken to crowds in the hundreds about the name and fame of Christ, I've started a few businesses that have impacted lives, I've created multiple platforms where

African and Caribbean men and women can share their stories in their own words and on their own terms, and I have a few notable awards and recognitions in the mix.

And no, I'm no Steven Furtick, Heather Lindsey, or TD Jakes. And no, my awards do not fit the classifications of a Grammy, an Oscar, a nod from Forbes, or a New York Times Bestseller. Having said this, if one is to search for someone who has done nothing of note or service in this life, they probably won't come looking for me.

Still, at 29, as alluded to in my messages to a person that I had never before met, I'm unfulfilled. I have responsibilities and obligations that keep me from pursuing the things I feel called to do and I constantly face intense opposition and obstacles in the pursuit of my goals. I'm tired, sometimes depressed, and frustrated. Needless to say, I'm not living the life I've dreamed of.

I know that I'm not alone. Conversations with my peers bring up very similar, if not equal, concerns. We wonder if we've been duped. We wonder if our big dreams – the ones we have been encouraged to pursue in fervency – are nothing but delusions. We often wonder if we will ever get to the destinations that have occupied the crevices of both our conscious and subconscious. We often wonder if the combination of our drive, ambition, and work ethic will ever lead us to their logical end; a manifestation of success, prosperity, and wealth. We often wonder if what we aspire to can be attained while we hold on to integrity and morality. We wonder. And on the evening of April 14th, I wondered.

My mental wanderings drove me. To conversation. With someone I really didn't know. A matter of great unusualness for me. You see, on the evening of the 14th of April, I had an encounter that drove me to a destination that perfectly encapsulates a sense of unfulfillment. Usually, the events after a visit to this place are characterized by a few days or weeks of depression; the kind which makes it a matter of difficulty for me to get out of bed and face life with any semblance of enthusiasm. However, this time around, I had a bit of a different response. I was frustrated, but the voice in my head was, unusually, not berating me or encouraging my frustration. It was saying something different from the other times. It was so clear to me that I even made it a post on my Facebook wall.

I've done the pit, I've been to the palace and been thrown in prison. In 2020, I'm saying, "Bye bye" to the holding cell. I will be called out of prison to govern.

I know, I know. This sounds like something a pastor would say at an Old Year's Night Service; sometimes right before the passing of an offering plate. This sounds like the typical New Year's Eve sermon where pastors seek to encourage and motivate their flock to make entrance into a new calendar year with hope and expectation. God knows I hate the sequence of events. And I promise you that I am a woman who is spiritually sober. Nonetheless, these are the words that greeted my frustration. And no, I had not been listening to any profound sermons in the days prior. No, I wasn't reading any motivational books. Truth be told, I had been wallowing in an abyss of self-pity and had seldom been in the Word as a good Christian should. This came out of nowhere.

Anyhoo, immediately after I shared this status on Facebook, I felt compelled to open up my Bible to the story of Joseph. If there is a story that I know well, it's this dreamer's story. I know it so well that there was no need for me to even Google the scriptural reference, as is a matter of custom when I am unsure of references. I know that the genesis of the story is found in Genesis Chapter 37, and that's exactly where I landed.

I know this story, but for reasons inexplicable, reading it this time around brought to light some previously unseen nuggets. Or maybe I had seen them in my previous readings, but they just had not yet resonated with me as they did at that moment.

As I delved deeper into the story, I also reflected on the people whose lives I admire; those who, in my estimation, have arrived at the destination of their dreams: The Steve Jobs-es, the Craig Groeschels, the Henry Kissinger's, the TD Jakes-es, the Kirk Franklins, the Alicia Keys, the Michael Jordans, the Lebron James-es, the Oprah Winfreys, and the A.W. Tozers. I recognized that NONE of them were overnight successes and that their stories tell of lives that have followed a blueprint not dissimilar from Joseph's.

From the very onset, Joseph was marked to become Egypt's governor. His destiny was set. He was favored with a gift that foreshadowed what was imminent. And as if that wasn't enough hinting, at 17, he was given a series of dreams – obnoxious and seemingly outrageous ones – that wouldn't show forth as reality until 13 years later. As a matter of fact, very few things about the string of events that followed the dreams which Joseph had been given suggested that he was on the path to, or near their fulfillment.

Thrown into a pit?

Sold into slavery?

Thrown into prison?

Who's bowing down to a slave?

At one point, Joseph did make entry into an arena that teased him of what was to come, but for the most part, although it was anything but, his rise seemed sudden. In hindsight, every *single* experience – even the ones which seemed to be so far-fetched from both the purpose which was previously foreshadowed and the prophecies which his dreams spake – was important and necessary.

The story of Joseph is a timeless classic, and in an age where more than ever we are encouraged to pursue all of our crazy, outrageous, world-changing, world-impacting dreams, it couldn't be more relevant.

A huge reason for its relevance is that it so prudently opposes the ethea of instant, quick, and accelerated that is of centrality to our present-day value system. In so doing, it serves as both a caution and an encouragement to the dreamer who feels that he or she is distant from fulfilling their dreams. "You'll get there," it says. "Slow down a little. Process is important. This is not the end," are all whispers emanating from the story if we take the time to listen carefully.

The story also gives its reader an edge. That we are given a bird's eye view of so many of the things which happened from start to finish, we can make certain gleanings that someone traversing the journey for the first time cannot. Many of the lessons we glean from Joseph's story today would only have been available to him in hindsight. But we have access NOW. Today. And we perish not, for knowledge is ours.

We all have goals, dreams, and aspirations. They are huge, beyond our understanding, and requisite of copious amounts of faith. Many of them will take us down paths unexpected, and during this trek, at certain points, some of us will find large amounts of our rest in the bosoms of frustration, depression, and confusion. That's where I am today, and many share a common space with me. However, after reading Joseph's story, I believe I have a better, often overlooked, understanding of what the journey to fulfilled dreams looks like, so I write.

dreamer. is the consideration of how one man's life has provided for us a clear reality of what the journey to fulfilled dreams looks like: process. And, Yes. Even in the 21st. century.

I don't know that Joseph's story will keep us fully from being lost, wandering, wondering, and discouraged, but I believe that for those who embrace its wisdom, the difficulties, strains, and faithlessness along, no doubt, what is an uncertain journey will be mitigated. Someone has gone before us, and it's been documented. We can learn what he did well, and we can also learn from what he didn't do well.

As I see it, the purpose of Joseph's story is to assist us in "getting understanding".

How do we determine what dreams are worthy?

What do we do with our dreams?

Do we even pursue them?

What are some of the experiences/challenges that we may face on the journey to realizing our dreams?

What roles will people play on this journey?

Are we on the right track?

The above are some of the questions that I believe "dreamer." will help provide the answers for.

For some, what I write here may not be a matter of novelty, but it may be a much-needed refresher. For others, it will change how they now view the experiences they've had or are having and will strengthen them to continue on a journey that may oftentimes seem like a difficult and hopeless road. For another set, **dreamer.** will completely blow their minds and turn their worlds around. I hope for all, **dreamer.** is a transporter of enveloping peace and understanding, and an encouragement that the journey to fulfilled dreams, amidst all the difficulties and trials, leads to one destination: Purpose fulfilled.

And what's a life without purpose?

the favored child.

3 Jacob[a] loved Joseph more than any of his other children because Joseph had been born to him in his old age. So one day Jacob had a special gift made for Joseph—a beautiful robe.[b] 4 But his brothers hated Joseph because their father loved him more than the rest of them. They couldn't say a kind word to him.

-

Genesis 37: 3-4 (NLT)

Growing up on a 238-square-mile island with a strong colonial past, I know and understand favoritism all too well. On an island whose population is characterized by a predominance of African descendants, it was not unusual for particular children to get the best parts in the choir or play simply because they carried skin a few hues lighter than melanin. There were also instances where children were treated better than others simply because of their parents' occupations or the suggestions of social status put forth by the contents of their lunchboxes.

In my teenage years, I saw favoritism in practice when dark-skinned women like myself were passed over or deemed less desirable by our male counterparts in favor of "*shabine*"[1], "*dougla*[2]" or mixed-race women. These judgments were made based solely on the perceived merit of the color of our skin or the texture of our hair. Needless to say, observing these things, growing up, I despised favoritism. Today, my tune has changed key. Just a little. I no longer despise favoritism. I haven't grown to love it, but I've grown to understand its place in the grand scheme of things.

---

[1]Saint Lucian Kwéyòl for a red-skinned woman. In his famed poem, Schooner, Saint Lucian Nobel Laureate, Derek Walcott references him self as "*Shabine*".

[2]Pronounced, *doe-gla,* this is Caribbean parlance for a man/woman of Indian and African heritage.

I've grown to understand that each of us is favored in our own way for various reasons and seasons. I've grown to realize that favor is not for the sake of the favored as much as it is for the fulfillment of divine purpose. The things I've grown to understand could not be more evident than they are in Joseph's story.

Jacob had 12 sons, of whom Joseph was the 11th; the one before the last. However, very early on in this story, we are told that Joseph was loved by his father more than his brothers. His father loved his brothers, but his father loved him more. His father loved him so much that he had a special gift made for him; a beautiful robe, described in the King James Version of the Bible as a **"coat of many colors" (Genesis 37:31, KJV)**. This robe, even before Joseph had been given a dream, was a point of contention between him and his brothers, and in hindsight, it foreshadows what would come.

Now, when one reads through Joseph's story in its entirety, one may be compelled to cast aside and label as trivial the intricate role of favor here in favor [pun intended] of the more hard-hitting or riveting parts. To many, the stories of his brother's reactions to his dreams, his being thrown into a pit, his being sold into slavery, and his going to prison for a crime that he did not commit are all far more exciting than talking about Joseph's continuous encounters with favor. But in Joseph's story, there are no trivial details. For this reason, this chapter is set to reveal the ways in which the favor we each carry is intricately intertwined with our unique journeys, leading us toward the realization of our dreams and ultimately guiding us to fulfill our intended purpose.

YOUR FATHER HAS FAVORED YOU WITH A GIFT

2 This is the account of Jacob and his family. When Joseph was seventeen years old, he often tended his father's flocks. He worked for his half brothers, the sons of his father's wives Bilhah and Zilpah. But Joseph reported to his father some of the bad things his brothers were doing.

-

Genesis 37:2 (NLT)

On Joseph's journey to purpose fulfilled, a story between a father and his beloved child is a central theme. As it is central to Joseph's story, so it is central to your journey to fulfilling your purpose.

Your Father has favored you with a gift.

One may be inclined to believe that in this instance, we speak of Jacob's gift to Joseph – a coat of many colors – but there is an even grander love and favor evident in Joseph's story. At the genesis of Joseph's journey, the story isn't so much about Joseph and Jacob as it is about Joseph and God. All this to say that while Jacob blessed his son with tangible, material gifts, God FIRST blessed Joseph with tremendous gifts; gifts of an immaterial and intangible persuasion.

Starting from the second verse of his story – well before Jacob's favor toward Joseph is introduced – we are told that, "Joseph reported to his father some of the bad things his brothers were doing". From this account, it is clear that Joseph showed an inclination toward management and overseeing very early on. He owned a spirit of excellence. He had the desire to see things done in the right way and to ensure that "owners" and "leaders" got the absolute best out of their estates and those of whom they had left in charge of these estates. This God-given gift would stay with Joseph throughout his lifetime, and it is that gift, amongst others – his looks (according to the Scriptures, the man was fine), his spirit of excellence, and the ability to see (vision) – that would propel him to the heights of influence in a foreign land.

So what has God blessed you with?

Some He has blessed with the ability to speak in the courts of queens and kings, and others He blessed with the ability to interpret and support the dreams of others. Some He has blessed with beauty undeniable, and others He endowed with unsurpassable genius. And it may be inflammatory to say this in a world so volatile and reverent to political correctness, but in some cases, your gift is the color of your skin, the color of the irises of your eyes, the length of your hair, the passport you hold or the family you were born into.

The gift may be a physical trait: timeless beauty, statuesque height and posture, beautiful skin, beautiful eyes, long eyelashes, unbelievably long legs, or even your skin tone.

The gift may be a character or personality trait: the ability to persevere or suffer long, the patience of Job, the ability to make everyone in a room feel comfortable, or in Joseph's case, the ability to see (vision) and manage well.

The gift may be a skill or a talent: you may be a gifted writer, orator, poet, thinker, musician, artist, singer, designer, carpenter, cleaner, mason, plumber, electrician, seamstress, tailor, actor, or athlete.

Whatever it may be, the journey to fulfilled dreams begins with a gift; a testament of your Father's – God's – favor on your life.

What has He favored you with?

You may believe that these gifts were only given to the Michael Jordans, Usain Bolts, LeBron James-es, Israel

Houghtons, Kirk Franklins, T.D. Jakes-es, Naomi Campbells, Ed Sheerans, Dr. Dres, Kanye West-es, Oprah Winfreys, Steve Jobs, Bill Gates or Barak Obamas of this world. But they were also given to you. You may believe that gifts are only given to a select few, but I believe that EVERY human being has been given a gift. Still, if you hold firmly enough to the philosophy that these gifts are reserved for a select few, consider that you are part of the elite few.

You have been favored by your Father.

You have been given a gift.

THE FAVOR OF MAN

3 Jacob[a] loved Joseph more than any of his other children because Joseph had been born to him in his old age. So one day Jacob had a special gift made for Joseph—a beautiful robe.

-

Genesis 37: 3 (NLT)

Jacob's storyline as a father presents him as a sub-type of God. His love for Joseph is symbolic of God's fatherly love toward us, His children. But also consider that it is symbolic of the favor of one man to another man. Ultimately, truthfully, Jacob is a mere man who has favored his son,

Joseph, another man, with responsibility and a robe fit for kings.

In addition to the gifts which God favors you with, you may also find that you are favored by men. This is not a favor that you would have positioned yourself to attain, nor is this a favor that you would have sought or chased after. For reasons unknown to you, for simply being you, you will find yourself in places where men – humans – will favor you.

You may consistently find yourself in positions where people expose you to their high-value networks, while others may find themselves in positions where people are always willing to invest in their projects or assignments. You may have the ability to pick up and go to any country in the world because no matter where you find yourself, there are people who will freely open up their homes to you. It may also mean that you consistently find people who will place you in strategic or influential positions even though you do not hold the traditional statuses, qualifications, experiences, or background that would qualify you.

Whatever it is, take note of the ways in which men favor you, for the combination of...

YOUR GIFT & YOUR PORTION OF FAVOR FORESHADOW YOUR DESTINATION

So Pharaoh commissioned Joseph: "I'm putting you in charge of the entire country of Egypt." Then Pharaoh removed his signet ring from his finger and slipped it on Joseph's hand. He outfitted him in robes of the best linen and put a gold chain around his neck. He put the second-in-command chariot at his disposal, and as he rode people shouted "Bravo!"

-

Genesis 41:41-43 (MSG)

If we were to be transported back to the times in which Joseph lived out this story, we'd likely find every Jewish man wearing a coat/robe. It was part of their daily wardrobe. It was part of the style and fashion of the time. It was what was swag, hip, and trendy. All this to say that Joseph being given a robe wasn't the issue of contention with his brothers. The issue was that Joseph was given a "special" robe.

Placing the knowledge that coats/robes were not an unusual part of the Jewish wardrobe alongside the *bacchanal*[3] which ensued after he was given the robe, we can

---

[3]The word *bacchanal* did not originate in the Caribbean. However it is embedded in the vernacular of several Caribbean countries, referencing/ describing trouble of epic and dramatic proportions; nasty business.

rightly surmise that Joseph's robe was definitively a robe out of the ordinary.

Researchers and scholars have suggested that it may have been longer than the knee-length tunics often worn. They have also suggested that the colorful fabric with which this robe was made was expensive and out of the ordinary; one fit for nobility and kings. And that may have been so, because callously, in doling out his punishment, his brothers tore it from him, almost as if to say, "We are stripping you from any notions that you will lead and we will bow".

If I'm making the case, I will say with definition, "Joseph's robe was a revelation of Joseph's destiny". He was a man who would lead. And as if to confirm this, when Pharaoh recognized that God was with him, he outfitted him in **"robes of the best linen"**.

YOU WILL BE MOCKED AND TREATED UNKINDLY

Usually, when our generation imagines occupying a space of favor or being drenched with giftedness, it accompanies an errant belief; the belief that favor equates a consistent state of fame, respect, honor, or being well-liked with little to no adverse or trying experiences. But this is oftentimes far from the reality. In reality, people who will change their worlds often find themselves in a space where many looking in will utter unkind words to and about them; about their gift, character, or personality.

And so it was with Joseph.

Joseph's brothers, recognizing the favor which rest upon his life, could not speak peaceably unto him or utter a kind word to him.

But his brothers hated Joseph because their father loved him more than the rest of them. They couldn't say a kind word to him.

-

Genesis 37:4 (NLT)

They tormented him, made his life a living hell, and probably mocked him every chance they got. They had already questioned the absurdity of his dreams which prophesied that they, who came before him, would bow before him, and when they plotted his demise, they scornfully referred to him as "that dreamer".

It is important to note that whatever dream has been given to you, you will be expected to journey to its realization in the midst of the evil of mankind. Yes, you will experience favor from some men, but you will without question be met with mockery and unkindness from others.

Don't worry. It's all part of the plan. Don't sweat it because…

YOU ARE QUALIFIED

In the 21st. century, perhaps a testament to the progression of human thought, we have a generation of people who will love and marry across borders, races, and tracks. But back in the day? Genealogies played an important role in positioning and valuing people. Even today, they continue to play an important role in positioning and valuing people. For example, if you were the son of a prisoner or criminal, it would be a very unlikely matter that you were married off to the King's daughter. I think *plenty wahala[4]* caricatures the fruit of such a scenario. It was also a matter that if a family sought to use marriage to advance their cause or wealth, they would seek to marry off their sons or daughters to the first in line to the throne and not necessarily the last born. I said all this to illustrate that traditionally, there is no principle or reason which supports why Joseph was the one to receive his father's favor.

In accordance with Jewish tradition, the firstborn son would be expected to carry on family leadership and would usually be the one to receive any such honor or treatment

---

[4]West African word used to describe trouble of epic and dramatic proportions.

akin to that which was bestowed upon Joseph. Yet, we are told that it is not the first, second, or even third-born son who is receiving this favor. We are told that Joseph is 11th in line.

Joseph's birth order, paralleled against his destiny, is valuable to understanding how God sometimes works in the grand scheme of things. It is purposeful in its insight to the person who may feel like their position in life limits them from accessing our Father's favor.

I've seen giftedness in many men and women, old and young – giftedness that so profoundly affects me that I point it out to the owner of the gift – and in several instances where I've pointed out these gifts, the owners were either unaware of them or they were not wearing them. Among other reasons, this [them not wearing it] often finds its root in a personal belief that something about them excludes them from receipt or worthiness of the gifts that have so graciously been given to them by their Father.

You may feel like the ability you've been given should be reserved only for those born in a particular country or form part of a particular socio-economic bracket. I can't tell you the number of times I've told myself, or someone in my circle has told me, "Saint Lucia [my homeland] too small for you, girl". The idea is that I can only be the fullness of myself or giftedness in another geographic location.

You may believe that your sex/gender disqualifies you from sitting in certain positions or that your ethnic background precludes you from certain opportunities. But I think Joseph's reaction to his Father's favor is instructive as to how we all should receive our gifts and what we should do with them. He wore it. Even in the presence of those who thought it was too much or that he felt he was *too big*.

With that said…

WEAR THE GIFT

So when Joseph arrived, his brothers ripped off the beautiful robe he was wearing.

-

Genesis 37:23 (NLT)

When Joseph was given his special robe, he could have easily and justifiably said, "You see me, boy, I eh wearing dis ting you know. 'Dem fellas already doe like my head. Lemme just pack dis ting in a corner and play it safe", but he didn't. Joseph wore his robe.

It's existed almost as long as the existence of humanity: Many are given gifts by our Father and opt not to wear them for fear that they will offend those who see them. But wearing the gift is important.

For one, it says to the giver that you are appreciative of the gift, but it is also a sign of acceptance of the destiny assigned to the gift. When you wear the gift, you prepare yourself for the destination which it foreshadows; you subconsciously internalize the promise that it holds, and it sets things in motion to carry you to second-in-command in Egypt.

Imagine being a young woman from a difficult, impoverished background, but you're gifted. You're gifted with a beautiful voice that rivals Whitney Houston and Patti LaBelle's put together, but you NEVER sing. This gift has the potential to take you and your entire family out of poverty, but it doesn't, because you NEVER sing. It is NEVER worn, and as such, it does not fulfill its purpose.

Can you imagine what would happen if Michael Jordan had never worn his cloak of perseverance? I can. And let me tell you, imagining a world where I can't hop on to YouTube to be inspired by video documentaries of poetry in motion on a basketball court or odes to the man's greatness is not a great one at all.

Can you imagine what the sport of track and field would have been like without the contributions of Usain Bolt?

Can you imagine what the NBA in 2020 would have been like if LeBron James had simply opted to not use his ability to hoop?

Can you imagine not having "If Only You Knew" or "Songs in A minor" if Patti LaBelle or Alicia Keys had neglected to wear their gifts?

Can you imagine never having heard Celine Dion's voice?

Can you imagine NOT having 12 quality studio albums from Kirk Franklin to carry you through life's dark days?

Can you imagine not having your precious MacBook or Surface Pro if Steve Jobs or Bill Gates had opted not to wear their gifts?

Understand this: The gift which your Father has given to you sets you apart. Whenever you wear it, wherever you wear it, people will see it. It pops. It is a "coat of many colors" and, therefore, cannot take on the glow of obscurity. Some will embrace it, but some will also be offended by what it means. Still, wear the gift or forsake the destiny.

the dream.

5 One night Joseph had a dream, and when he told his brothers about it, they hated him more than ever. 6 "Listen to this dream," he said. 7 "We were out in the field, tying up bundles of grain. Suddenly my bundle stood up, and your bundles all gathered around and bowed low before mine!" 9 Soon Joseph had another dream, and again he told his brothers about it. "Listen, I have had another dream," he said. "The sun, moon, and eleven stars bowed low before me!" 10 This time he told the dream to his father as well as to his brothers, but his father scolded him. "What kind of dream is that?" he asked. "Will your mother and I and your brothers actually come and bow to the ground before you?" 11 But while his brothers were jealous of Joseph, his father wondered what the dreams meant.

-

Genesis 37:5-7, 9-11 (NLT)

A few days before my 27th birthday, I sat to answer a few questions from a journalist interested in doing a piece on me and my work with Wakonté. She asked me, "Where do you see yourself in 10 years' time?"

It seems a simple enough question. However, it marked a rare occasion where I struggled to string words together. My destiny in 10 years' time wasn't something that I'd thought of; at least not in an ordered manner. I had dreamt a lot in my teens for my 20s, but I don't think I'd ever taken time to think deeply about life in my 30s. Notwithstanding, after some thought, I was able to come up with an answer, and I believe my response beautifully sums up my mission and my dream.

The response was so grand, so beyond me, and so crazy that after I read it, I questioned my sanity. It's a little over 5 years to the date since I answered that question, and the response is still shocking to me. It speaks of a profound end; an end profound for anyone but even more so for a little black girl from a small fishing village on an island reflected as a dot on the world map.

This was my response:

If I could design my life to perfection, in 10 years, I would be a New York Times Bestselling author and multimillionaire. I would be in the process of making significant academic and practical contributions to my areas of interest: international development (specifically African and Caribbean development), entrepreneurship, theology, faith, art, culture, music, sport, and the convergence of these varied interests. I would be a well-sought-after keynote speaker both within secular and Christian spheres, and I probably would be at the starting point of doing life with a gorgeous man, or I would have already begun the settling phase and well on my way to having a couple of children.

At the time, I didn't, but today you can throw branding and public service into the mix of this already compound vision, and there you have it: my BIG dream.

Now, you may be wondering why I'm sharing these things.

I shared my dream here for two reasons: The first is that when I read Joseph's story this time, the gleanings helped me understand why, on this journey to fulfilling the things which have been placed on my heart, I currently and often find rest on the streets of Frustration. The second reason will become evident as you continue to read; even more so when you come to the section titled, "What We Do With Dreams".

But back to this, here, point:

Joseph's dreams were extremely specific. In two different ways, at two different times, he learned of one outcome: people would bow before him.

The dreams spoke of elevation and power. They spoke of greatness and reign. They spoke of influence and desirable positions. They were beautiful but also left us with questions of whether dreams – good, wholesome, worthy dreams – are only those characterized by people bowing before us; power and glory. I answer this with three words…

DREAMS ARE BIG

Consider that good dreams are not only characterized by people bowing before us, but also consider that there are no small dreams.

Dreams are big.

I believe that the worthy dreams always result in one's elevation.

And allow this to be contextualized.

When you hop into a dictionary to find the meaning of the word dream, you will find the following list:

dream (noun), often attributive

1: a series of thoughts, images, or emotions occurring during sleep

had a *dream* about climbing a mountain

gives me bad *dreams*

— compare REM SLEEP

2: an experience of waking life having the characteristics of a dream: such as

a : a visionary (see VISIONARY entry 1 sense 2a) creation of the imagination : DAYDREAM

the *dreams* of her youth

b: a state of mind marked by abstraction or release from reality : REVERIE

walking around in a *dream*

c : an object seen in a dreamlike state : VISION

a man that was her *dream* come true

3: something notable for its beauty, excellence, or enjoyable quality

the new car is a *dream* to operate

4

a : a strongly desired goal or purpose

a *dream* of becoming president

b: something that fully satisfies a wish : IDEAL

a meal that was a gourmet's *dream*

By its very definition, a dream is something not easily

attainable. A dream speaks of an ideal place or position. A dream speaks to something different from the norm. A dream speaks of a space that contradicts mundane and ordinary realities. Thus, if it is someone's "dream", it is big. It is significant. If it is a dream for someone, it will require toil, dedication, hope, faith, sacrifice, and pain.

This is for the dreamer who may have been told that whatever he or she dreamt is too small or not enough. This is for the dreamer whose only desire is to own a decent 3-bedroom home and not the penthouse at an expensive high-rise building. To this dreamer, 3 bedrooms with space to accommodate visits from friends, parents, and siblings is an unprecedented luxury after spending years living on the streets and sleeping in the trunks of old cars. This is for the dreamer whose ONLY big desire is to have a lasting marriage founded on respect and friendship. You see, this dreamer grew up in a home that afforded every luxury a child could think of, except a mother and father who loved and respected each other.

When we evaluate dreams from this perspective, we can only conclude that if it is a dream, it is significant.

This is not to say that one should reject calls to dream bigger, or more prominently, but it is to say that if someone beholds or calls something a "dream", it is no small feat.

This is not to say that one's capacity to dream will never be expanded, but this is to say that if it is your dream, it requires unknown, divine strength to traverse the journey that will bring you to its fulfillment.

Dreams are big.

YOUR DREAM WON'T REVEAL A CUSTOM MAP FOR YOUR JOURNEY. START LIVING.

Joseph's dream prophesied a particular end: His brothers, and even his father, would bow before him. That was it. That was all. Nothing more. Nothing less.

The dreams never foretold that their details would only come to pass 13 years after they were given. The dreams never foretold that Joseph would be thrown into a pit, sold into slavery, sent to prison, spend years in Egypt or even rule over Egypt. The dreams revealed ONE thing: Joseph's brothers and father would bow before him.

One of the most frustrating things for dreamers is that they very rarely see the journey that will carry them to the fulfillment of their dreams. They often do not even understand what impact their vision will have on their generation or the generations to come. They see a grandiose end of accolades, money, wealth, power, or influence, but they very rarely see the pit, slavery, or prison.

Steve Jobs had a particular dream about the kind of company that he wanted to build. He was a great visionary with the ability to get people excited and postured toward the attainment of a difficult-to-accomplish reality, but I'm almost certain that he never envisioned not always being a part of Apple's senior management during his lifetime. He didn't know that some of his colleagues would grow so sick of the way he spoke to and treated them that they would take the necessary steps to get him booted out of his own company. The dream never showed him that being kicked out of Apple would lead him to Pixar. The dream never revealed that his fall from grace would carve out a path necessary to his understanding of how to create grand experiences; how to bring dying companies back to life. The dream never showed him that being kicked out of his own company would provide him with knowledge on entertainment, peer to none, that would see him transform Apple into a company that produced more than just computers. The dream never showed him the turmoils and the trials he would endure on the journey to making Apple one of the world's most renowned brands.

LeBron James had, and still holds, a dream of becoming one of the greatest basketball players to ever walk the earth. Very early on, he knew that his salary, alongside lucrative endorsement deals, would help him take his family out of poverty, but at the time, he didn't know that it would be years before he got his first ring. He didn't know that leaving the team which drafted him as the #1 overall pick into the NBA would cause untold media uproar. He didn't know that he would become one of the most scrutinized ball players in the history of the game. He didn't know of the strain and responsibility that would come with being the best. He probably didn't realize that his dream to become one of the best basketball players the world has ever had the privilege of witnessing would lead him to send thousands of children to college. He didn't know that his stature would see him playing a critical role in the activism and politics of today.

When I listen to T.D. Jakes' story of his journey, the one which has led to him becoming one of the most sought-after speakers of our generation, I marvel that this man once walked with shoes that had holes in them. I marvel that at the beginning of his journey as a preacher, he commanded an audience of less than 50. It's hard to believe, and it's very likely that God didn't whisper in his ear that this would be the path to his crown.

Michael Jordan's journey to becoming inarguably the greatest basketball player of all time was a tumultuous one. He was drafted third overall in the 1984 NBA Draft, coming off a winning season at Chapel Hill. There were great expectations, but it would take 6 years before he would win his first NBA title.

As for me, I expected nothing of what my journey has been. I expected my path to have some bumps, but not many. I was going to become a hotshot lawyer, ruthless in all my ways, with a beautiful corner office and multiple press conferences detailing how I'd soundly beaten my opponents. But here I am...

After the dream, many of us seek knowledge of the journey or more detailed maps in the stead of simply living. We want to know. We wish to move forward without making any errors or facing any hardships. Knowing what I know now, I believe that not seeing the details of the journey or map beforehand is how God has purposefully designed things. It is possible that if we are given full disclosure, revelation, or knowledge of what it will take to get to what we see in our dreams, many of us would forsake the grandiose end for a life of comfort: a life without the pit, a life without haters, struggles, untruthful accusations, and prison. So not seeing every detail of the map – every house or every tree along the way – is God's plan.

So, if we can't see every detail on the map, what's next?

As is the example of Joseph, after the dream has been deposited within the vessel that is you or I, the next step is simply to keep living: keep being a mom, keep being a dad, keep working that 9-5, keep mentoring young men and women, keep speaking as the opportunity arises, keep leading your failing youth group, keep saving, keep preparing, keep writing, keep producing music, keep growing that company, keep living. You will find that it is in living that our *journeys* unfold. As you read through the latter chapters, you will find that it is in living that *purpose* unfolds. As you read through later chapters, you will find that it is in dealing with all of what life throws at us – the ups, the downs, the highs, and the lows – that we draw closer and closer to the manifestation of our dreams.

So you asked, "What's next?"

Start living. Keep living.

YOUR DREAM WILL SERVE OTHERS MORE THAN IT SERVES YOU

Joseph's story doesn't tell us specifically his thoughts about his dreams, so it cannot definitively be said that Joseph was excited to behold the influence/power that would come with the fulfillment of the dream. Still, the story tells us that he spoke of the dreams in a way that annoyed his brothers. So I'm going to put myself in his shoes, and perhaps you too can join me in this brief moment of active imagination.

At 17 years old, given two dreams which spake of greatness, rule, reign, and power, I would have been super excited to be ushered into that reality. And I think that by the way Joseph spoke of the dreams – annoyingly – he probably was too. What he didn't know was that the dreams would serve others far more than they served him.

Pshhshwhwhshhhw....(This is meant to be the typed expression of the sound you hear when you fast-forward a tape recorder). So fast forwarding...

After Joseph had sat in prison for a few years, an opportunity came to him. He would interpret some of Pharaoh's dreams and be made ruler over Egypt, second in his power and influence only to Pharaoh. For seven years, he commandeered an entire nation to store well for an approaching season of famine. This opportunity would bring him to the fulfillment of his dreams: his brothers and father bowing before him. However, the end would be minute compared to how his dream had served the nations of the world. According to verse 57 of the 39th Chapter of the book of Genesis **"...people from all around came to Egypt to buy grain from Joseph because the famine was severe throughout the world."(NLT)**

Joseph was unaware that his brothers would fulfill the prophecies of his dream while they were on a quest for food in a season of famine. Joseph was unaware that he would become second-in-command in a foreign land. Joseph did not know that he would design and commandeer the world's largest food trading hub. Joseph was without knowledge that the events of the dream were far less significant than the service it would render to legions of people.

In the end, the dream wasn't so much about Joseph's father and brothers bowing before him. In the end, the dream wasn't so much about the air of luxury which accompanied expensive robes, nor was it about the jewelry that would be restored to him. In the end, we see explicitly that the dream was about saving people and saving nations. In the end, we see that the dream saved – possibly millions – of people from dying of starvation.

And now don't be worried or angry with yourselves for selling me here, because God sent you ahead of me to preserve life.

–

Genesis 45:5 (NLT)

Many of us often feel like our dream or vision is about us. We errantly believe that it is about our progress, our wealth, our sake, our name, our fame or our success, but just like Joseph's dream, we will find out that our dreams are meant to serve others more than they serve us. Just like Joseph's dream, our dreams will serve others more than it serves us.

WHAT WE DO WITH DREAMS

⁹Soon Joseph had another dream, and again he told his brothers about it. "Listen, I have had another dream," he said. "The sun, moon, and eleven stars bowed low before me!" ¹⁰This time he told the dream to his father as well as to his brothers, but his father scolded him. "What kind of dream is that?" he asked. "Will your mother and I and your brothers actually come and bow to the ground before you?" ¹¹But while his brothers were jealous of Joseph, his father wondered what the dreams meant.

—

Genesis 37:9-11 (NLT)

If there is a lesson that many – even the most infrequent Bible reader – would purport to have gleaned from Joseph's story, it is the lesson of knowing what to do with dreams. They say that they have grasped the lesson about being careful who to share your dreams with or the one which says NOT to share your dreams with anyone at all.

"Roll in silence", they say.

"Be quiet about your next move", they say.

"Outside energy will throw your goals off", they say.

And yes, in some cases, these bits of advice may hold valuable. But is this really the lesson that we are to take from Joseph's story?

What are we really supposed to do with our dreams?

Here are a few things I've gleaned from Joseph's blueprint.

1. BELIEVE AND BE OBSESSED

One of the things I admire most about Joseph is that he believed that his dreams were the real deal and would come to pass. His belief is evident in the repetition of his dreams and how he talked about them. These things, the repetition and the way he talked about them, also reflect what obsessed people do. They talk about their dreams with great fervor; passionately, and incessantly. It was this very passion and fervor with which Joseph spoke that annoyed his brothers. But he couldn't help it. He was utterly captivated by his dreams. He was excited about them. He wanted to understand what they meant with the utmost clarity. He gave them a central place in his thoughts and speech; he made them his focus.

Like Joseph, the dreamer who will see his or her dream to the end MUST believe unwaveringly in the vision that he/she has beheld. The dreamer who will see his or her dream to the end must examine the fullness of his/her visions. He/she must be captivated by the sheer beauty and or weight of the vision. Their dreams must occupy such significant space in their thoughts and in their speech, so much so that by the time they come to the attainment of them, the necessary characters in their unfolding and confirmation would have been well acquainted with them.

2. RECORD THE DREAM

I'm sure you've found yourself in this place of near-tangible frustration. At least once. And here's how it goes: You're in a state of deep sleep, but you're having the most exquisite, wild, and prophetic dream. You will preach to millions, you will sing to hundreds of thousands, you will have that corner office with the view. You will emerge a bestselling author with global tours. You will.

You arise from your slumber a few hours later, and deep within yourself you know, without a shadow of a doubt, that you just had a dream worthy of remembering, but you have forgotten all or most of the finer details. These details haunt you for weeks and weeks on end. You feel like you've lost something that is a part of you; something that should have given you peace of mind and even direction. Sometimes the details come back, but other times they are entirely lost.

Sometimes our dreams are in fact given to us during a time of sleep, and all we're left with are sketchy details with no replays. However, for many of us, the idea of the dream or vision presented here is a collection of desires, wishes, or visions that God continually places on our hearts and in our minds. When these leanings, proddings, and moments of clarity continually come, I believe that it is our duty to record them. These recordings are for posterity, but they also serve the purpose of carrying us through the difficult, dark, faith-low, and sometimes faithless days.

And so it was with Joseph.

As if to ensure that Joseph took notice of what had been deposited in him, he dreamt twice, and each time he told his brothers and father what he had dreamt. To many looking in, Joseph was being an ostentatious child with his head in the clouds, but retelling his dreams was important. The retelling served the purpose of recording his dreams. His repetition of the details served to implant them deeply on the crevices of his heart but they also served the purpose of creating witnesses to God's providence and omniscience when the things he had dreamt would eventually come to pass.

3. SHARE THE DREAM

I may be one of a tiny group of people whose prime takeaway from Joseph's story is not that dreams should not be shared. On the contrary, I took from the story that dreams ought to be shared.

Perhaps the lesson is that the practice of sharing must be undertaken with all wisdom. Perhaps the lesson is that one needs to be prayerful about discerning the right time to share a dream. Perhaps the lesson is that one needs to be careful how one speaks when one shares one's dreams so as not to incite feelings of inadequacy, smallness, lack of purpose, or jealousy in others. These lessons will bear the fruit of something that a young, enthusiastic Joseph lacked at the time: emotional intelligence. Having said this, emotional intelligence notwithstanding, I still glean that the message therein is to share the dream.

Even in its lack of emotional intelligence Joseph's sharing of his dreams was important, for in doing so, he set into motion many of the events that would carry him to Egypt, the destination of the fulfillment of his purpose.

And his brothers?

Though driven by hate and jealousy, they unknowingly assisted him in fulfilling his dreams.

Joseph's story also acquaints us with the dreams of others: the baker, the butler, and Pharaoh. In each of these instances, these dreamers sought to share their dreams with another. In each of these instances, these dreamers understood that the dreams given to them were so complex, so valuable to their dispensation, and had the potential for such far-reaching impact that they would need help interpreting them. In the same way, many of us will need to share our dreams in order for others to help us decode them, give meaning to them and bring them to life.

Dreams, because of their magnanimity, usually cannot be fulfilled in silos. They require partnership. They require wisdom and insight from others. They necessitate antagonists who provide conditions that build one's resilience and perseverance. And this is why sharing them is so important. Permit me to be bold in saying that an unshared dream has never been fulfilled.

I find it no mystery that Steve Jobs, as visionary as he was, found it a matter of necessity to share his dream of what Apple would become with several people. He first approached Wozniak, an electronics genius who would play an elemental role in creating the first set of Apple products. Some of the people he shared his dream with didn't understand. Some of them, like Joseph's brothers, felt that he was a young, arrogant man who didn't have his feet on the ground. Some of them, like Jacob, were puzzled, but they availed themselves and their resources and became his business partners, investors, and teammates. At the end of the day, everyone he shared his dream with played some kind of role in helping him build Apple.

This is why I've shared my "big dream" with you here. In my personal space, I've seen that not sharing has limited my movement. Sometimes in having a conversation with a random person, they are able to connect me with the right person or people to carry me forward. For example, I shared that I wanted to have Golda Lee Bruce[5] write the foreword for one of my books with someone who just happened to know her. I never imagined that he did. I was simply sharing, and just like that, he put me in touch with her. Just this morning, I approached someone to share with him part of my big dream, and he immediately postured himself to help me take it to where I desire for it to be. Who knows? Someone reading this book may shoot me an email or a WhatsApp message to share, with me, a bit of wisdom or information that will carry me to the next stage of my journey.

Seek wisdom from above always, but believe me, if you are to take up the responsibility of seriously stewarding a vision, at one point or another, you WILL share the dream.

---

[5] If you're here you'll know if I actually got her to write the Foreword.

empty cisterns.

23 So when Joseph arrived, his brothers ripped off the beautiful robe he was wearing. 24 Then they grabbed him and threw him into the cistern. Now the cistern was empty; there was no water in it.

—

Genesis 37:23-24 (NLT)

I went to a meeting with a list of deliverables, confident that I had met expectations, and at the end of the meeting, with not one deliverable discussed, I was without a job. In the name of full transparency, I've had this issue before: the issue where I come into a work environment with great excitement only to leave on a disappointing note. I've had this issue before, but this time around, about a month and a half away from my 29th birthday, I was a little pissed off. I felt two things: a bit like an empty cistern and like I had come to the point of empty cisterns in my journey.

Cisterns are vessels with huge capacity and potential. When they are fulfilling purpose they carry things, and oftentimes, in accordance with their purpose people expect things from them.

Shepherds expect to be able to draw from them to water their flock, farmers expect to be able to draw from them to water their crops, travelers see them as spots of refreshing, and nations see them as instrumental to preserving life during seasons of drought. So you see, cisterns are expected to carry valuable things and when they are found to be empty, any number of things can go wrong, rendering the pit a vessel of diminished use and value and thus available for sinister uses that deviate from its original purpose.

Joseph was no stranger to the reality of "empty cisterns". By about verse 21 of Chapter 37, Joseph has dreamt twice about his imminent rise – a rise which would be signaled by his brothers and father bowing before him – he has annoyingly shared each dream with his father and brothers, and he is sent on an assignment by his father. By about verse 21 of Chapter 37 the reader will make entrance into perhaps one of the most well-known parts of Joseph's story: the part where he is thrown into an empty cistern.

Most have taught and believed that if Joseph had not shared his dream with his brothers that he would not have encountered the pit but is this really how he got thrown into that pit? How did he really get thrown into that pit?

AN ASSIGNMENT WILL LEAD YOU TO THE PIT

At verse 14 of Chapter 37, we are introduced to the genesis and makings of Joseph's low point, the pit. Jacob sends Joseph to check up on his older brothers – to, according to Caribbean parlance, *"mako*[6]*"* – and to bring back a report. Where I'm from, because of this assignment, Joseph would be considered nothing less than a prime *"sousè*[7]*"*. Where you're from, he would probably be seen as a *"snitch"* or a *"rat"*, and you may feel like you understand why this

---

[6] Pronounced *maa-co*, it is Caribbean parlance for a gossip, or someone who is inordinately concerned with another's affairs/business.

[7] Pronounced, *soo-sear*, it is a Saint Lucian Kwéyòl word to describe someone who reveals another person's business or functions as an informant or spy.

man-child just wasn't likable AT ALL. Whatever we may think of him, Joseph had all the makings of a diligent overseer.

Because of the gift of hindsight we can see that even though Jacob was not fully convinced and even shaken by the types of dreams which Joseph had, he would play a powerful and undeniable role in training him for his eventual position as overseer of Egypt. Jacob, in his actions, was encouraging Joseph to grow into his God-given ability of management and stewardship.

Okay. So maybe Joseph's decision to share his dreams had a role to play, but a deeper look at the story shows that there is a more direct link between Joseph being sent on an assignment by his father and his journey to the pit than there is to Joseph's decision to share his dreams and his journey to the pit. True, sharing his dreams caused his brothers to hate him even more than they already did, and it is that hate that gave fuel to their actions on that fateful day at Dothan, but they had hated him anyway. They hated him well before he shared his dreams. Furthermore, many– significant – things happen between Joseph's recounting of his dreams, and his being thrown into the pit.

The account tells us that at the behest of his father, Joseph travelled from Shechem to the valley of Hebron, where he believed his brothers would be. He got to the valley, but they were not there. His course of action could have been to return to his father and report that his brothers were no longer at the valley of Hebron, but in typical Joseph style – excellence, enthusiasm, and a desire to complete the task at hand – he persisted. He would not return to Jacob until he had seen his brothers and was able to give a report.

Joseph is eventually found wandering around the countryside by a man from the area and uses the opportunity to enquire about where his brothers could be found. The man directed him to Dothan. Again, Joseph could have chosen, at that point, to return to his father to inform him that his brothers had gone to Dothan, but to Dothan he went.

Many times when we find ourselves in a place of lowness on our journey, we often seek to find means to understand why we are where we are. Some of us believe that we have misstepped, some of us believe that we have taken the wrong paths, some of us believe that we shared our dreams with the wrong people, but the truth is that like Joseph, many of us will encounter this low point – the empty cistern – while on assignment. This is to say that we will encounter this place of lowness while we are doing exactly what we are to be doing. We will encounter this low place while walking in our giftings. We will encounter this low place on assignment given to us by our Father.

HATERS ARE NECESSARY

Scroll through any social media site or listen to a few popular songs, and you will likely see and hear the word *"hater"* a few times. Our generation is obsessed with haters. And while on the one hand they often speak of *"haters"* in a negative light, on the other hand, the existence of haters, or one having haters, is often seen as a stature symbol: You have some measure of talent, wealth, or beauty or you have attained something of great significance if people are *hating* on you.

When I examine Joseph's story integrally – from an integrated perspective as opposed to a compartmentalized perspective – I can come to only one conclusion: "Haters" are necessary to the fulfillment of one's destiny.

We know the end of the story. We know that Joseph would eventually become Egypt's second-in-command. We also know that Joseph got to Egypt because his brothers sold him; out of jealousy and hatred.

Could Joseph have gotten to Egypt through less antagonistic means? Absolutely. Still, the reality is that he got there because of his haters.

This realization is also why I preach that it is important to share your dreams. The reality is that no matter how selective we are in sharing our dreams, at some point in time, they will be shared with someone who doesn't want to see us rule or reign.

If you're an entrepreneur, through a simple press article highlighting the products/services that you have made available to your customers, what you're doing can come to the attention of a competitor who believes that they should be the one dominating the space that you have chosen to function in, and they could embark on a journey to discredit you.

If you're an athlete, you don't ever have to speak your dream to become a professional cricketer or to make it to the NBA or NFL to anyone for them to recognize what's happening. The way you carry yourself on the court or field, or the disciplined approach towards your craft will signal to people that this man or woman is serious about his business. And many, for various reasons, will scorn your ascendance.

In an ideal world, these recognitions ought not to attract anything other than fellow humans who are rooting for your success – others who are content to see you reflect the glory of God – but the fallen nature of mankind has made it so that sometimes your gifts, successes, and disposition will attract jealousy, envy and even hate.

But fear not, for God, in his omniscience has intended it for good, and in his omnipotence he will utilize their evil to positively impact the lives of many.

EMPTY CISTERNS ARE PLACES OF "JUXTAPOSITION"

At the place of juxtaposition, the events of your life will appear opposite to every promise you once held. Everything will look contrary to the dream or vision deposited within you. If you ask me, I'll say without hesitation that it is one of the most devastating places to be. It is a place of uncertainty, a place of being at the mercy of others, a place of pain, breaking, humility, submission, and weakness.

Joseph, a young man who had dreamt that he would rule and reign – a young man of promise – had now found himself in a position of utmost submission. He was at the mercy of the very men who would bow before him. His robe, which prophesied of an end of power and stature, had been stripped off him, and he was thrown into an empty cistern.

Many times in our journey, we arrive at places that look nothing like what we dreamed of. These places stand in stark contrast to our destination. We dreamt wealth and see poverty. We dreamt of professional success, yet we are unemployed or struggling in dead-end jobs. We dreamt of a happy, thriving, prosperous family, yet we see a troublesome spouse. But be not dismayed. Your low place is but a juxtaposition of your destination. You are merely at a step in your journey to purpose fulfilled. An impending season will bring you to exactly what you dreamt of.

YOU WILL NOT DIE

From all accounts, the empty cistern was meant to be the death of Joseph. His brothers first suggested killing him and throwing him into one of the cisterns, but Reuben intervened and said, "Let's leave him here and he will die without us touching him". Of course, we are told that Reuben had every intention of returning to rescue Joseph. Still, on two occasions, the empty cistern is cited as the place to eventually become home to Joseph's corpse.

Likewise, when you have found yourself in the place of empty cisterns, you will likely feel like it is the end of you. You may feel like you have come to the end of your dreams and aspirations; that they will never be realized. Some people suffer such deep depression that they no longer see value in their lives. But like Joseph, you will not die. It may be the end of yourself or your life as you know it, but it is not the death of you. Instead, you will transition.

But before that transition, note that…

YOU WILL LIVE BECAUSE OF REUBEN AND JUDAH

A large part of why Joseph survived the empty cistern is because there were interventions made on his behalf by two of his brothers: Reuben and Judah.

Without doubt, one of the nuggets to be taken from this is that in low periods, there will be people who will help you survive. Without doubt, we are being told that some brothers – or sisters – will come to our aid in our lowest seasons. But I think there is an even more profound lesson on what will facilitate and foster survival and life during the seasons of the empty cistern: Reuben and Judah.

REUBEN

Reuben is Jacob's firstborn son. His mother? His father's rejected and hurting wife, Leah.

Leah could never measure up to Jacob's love for Joseph's mother, Rachel. But she craved it. She craved his adoration. She craved his attention. And though it still couldn't compare to being covered in a love freely given, she believed that she could be of some value to Jacob if she could bear him sons. This belief was further heightened because through birthing sons, she could do something which a barren Rachel couldn't. With contention and strife brewing in Jacob's camps, Leah gave birth to their first son and named him Reuben.

According to Jewish etymology the name Reuben is made up of two words: "re'u" which means "look" or "see," and "ben" which means "son." Jewish rabbis say that the name Reuben expresses Leah's elation that "re'u"– G-d had seen her needs –her affliction and misery – and therefore blessed her with "ben" – a son. It would not be amiss to say that in this case, Leah saw her son as a salve or salvation from Jacob's disregard and minimization of her. From this account, we see that Reuben continued to be this for others, more specifically Joseph.

The etymology is important here because it demonstrates that the first intervention during Joseph's low season came via Reuben; it came because the Lord saw his afflictions and blessed him with a Son/Salve.

Oftentimes when you are on this journey, if you believe in a higher power[8], you will be tempted to ask, "Where is God in all this?" Surely, God, in His omniscience and omnipotence would not allow you to go through such perplexities and quagmires. However, if there is anything I've taken from Joseph's story, it is that the journey is not one designed to be bereft of trials or difficulties. In the

---

[8] And sometimes even when you don't. * *

midst of these challenges, be encouraged that God hears and sees your misery, your affliction and your difficulty.

For me, this etymological revelation is a reminder that in some of the most difficult, uncomfortable seasons of my life, I remain with breath and hope, and it is so because God sees and hears my afflictions.

JUDAH

The next person who intervened on Joseph's behalf was Leah's fourth and last son, Judah. Examining the etymology behind his name also brings us to revelation kin in beauty to that which exploring the etymology of Reuben's name brings us.

After Leah gave birth to Reuben, 3 more times, she bore Jacob sons, and each time she named them in reflection of a season she was enduring or had endured. When she bore Judah, she felt that God had sufficiently blessed her that she would praise him, and so she called her fourth son, Judah, meaning, "Now I will praise the Lord".

There is probably now no requirement for me to expound on this further, but I will.

In challenging seasons and times, our praise – a disposition of gratitude to God – will play an elemental role in keeping us alive.

There is no Biblical exposition on what Joseph did while he was in the pit. We don't know if he was scared and trembling. We don't know if he was strong and hopeful. We don't know if he curled up in a corner and wet his pants.

We.

Don't.

Know.

At least not for sure.

Nevertheless, I think it of great importance that we were told who intervened to save his life. I think it no coincidence that the ones who intervened were Reuben and Judah.

Come on, somebody. Touch your neighbour and say, "You will live because of Reuben and Judah".

Okay. Okay. I play too much. But this was a word: You will live because of Reuben and Judah.

You will live because God sees and hears your affliction; He will send you a son; a savior.

You will live because of Praise.

the transition.

23 So when Joseph arrived, his brothers ripped off the beautiful robe he was wearing. 24 Then they grabbed him and threw him into the cistern. Now the cistern was empty; there was no water in it.

-

Genesis 37:23-24 (NLT)

After a low point – after that low point where your life flashes before your eyes, and you are at the mercy of others – the next step is almost always transition. Some of us mark it with a new haircut or new hairstyle, we revamp the digs in our wardrobes, we move out of our parents' homes into our own apartments, we move to new cities, states, countries, and continents, we start college, a new job or even get married or divorced. For many, these moments are marked by joy, elation, and hope, but they are almost always wrapped in with their polar opposites: fear, anxiety, and apprehension.

We don't know if our new cut or new hairstyle is going to fit the shape of our head or the shape of our face well. We're not entirely sure how we will eat healthy meals every day without the support of our parents or siblings to chop the seasonings alongside us. We're unsure how well we'd like the people or the food in a new city, country, or state. We're not sure how well we'll be able to tolerate the constant presence of a spouse. We're unsure how we will cope with being the only parent home with the kids after a 12-year marriage. But still, there is a hope that things are going to be better than the empty cistern which had almost claimed our lives.

Joseph's brothers intended for the pit to mark the end of his life, but the continuation of his story tells us that he did not die. Instead, we are told that he was carried through a few steps of transition. As I look at the happenings that compose Joseph's transition season, I see many lessons and experiences that anyone pursuing the journey to fulfilled dreams – purpose – will encounter. One is likely to experience all or a selection from the following[9]:

1. the experience of being undervalued or devalued
2. the experience of losing your robe.
3. the experience of those closest to you believing that you are lost/dead,
4. the entry into a place that suggests that you are finally where you should be, then,
5. the test of faith and integrity that will end the season of transition and carry you to prison.

So here we go. First things, first. There's no escaping it…

YOU WILL MAKE THE TREK TO EGYPT

But when Reuben heard of their scheme, he came to Joseph's rescue. "Let's not kill him," he said. "Why should we shed any blood? Let's just throw him into this empty cistern here in the wilderness. Then he'll die without our laying a hand on him." Reuben was secretly planning to rescue Joseph and return him to his father.

–

Genesis 37:21-22(NLT)

---

[9]For better elucidation, points 4 and 5 will be dealt with in a subsequent Chapter called, "teased".

In the first draft of the book, I left this section out, but returned to add it in one of the more final drafts. My return occurred at a point where I had become friends with a niggling feeling that said that this may be important to someone who's learning not to be mad at the world for their troubles.

The truth is that some people want to help you, but because they must preserve themselves, their families, or their status in their space, they are unable to help in a manner that is timely. And we see this in Joseph's story.

Reuben had every intention of returning to save Joseph from the pit. However, he did not want to do so in a manner that would damage his alliance with the remainder of his brothers, so he decided to leave Joseph in the pit until he could return, quietly, to release him. But it was not to be, because Joseph was gone by the time he got back.

Along your journey to fulfilling purpose, you will encounter a few Reubens. This means that you will encounter a few people who will desire to rescue you – save you from a particular fate – but will be unable to do so in a timely fashion. That's probably because you MUST make the trek to Egypt.

I remember losing a full tuition scholarship to do law in the UK in 2015. I required a particular sum of money to secure my student visa, and while I had the means to secure the funds via loan and was in the process of doing so, the bank was taking forever. They took long enough that I lost the scholarship. They approved the loan 3 weeks after the required date. But before that, I recognized their delays, and I was hoping that someone would be able to front the money to me until the loan came through. I asked, and unfortunately, no one was able to help. I was devastated. I had always wanted to become this hotshot lawyer, but the dream was gone. A few months after the fact, a family friend who heard that I lost the scholarship was disappointed that she hadn't known earlier because she had the means to help, but the opportunity was no more.

In 2018 an investor wanted to bankroll Wakonté. We found ourselves as far as convening in New York, ready to seal the deal, and then boom, he found himself in a position where he was unable to do what was promised. I left New York with no investment in hand.

Not too long ago, someone wanted to help me acquire the necessary funding to bring two ed-techs to life; two ed-techs that would play a huge role in helping to provide high school-aged students across West Africa and the Caribbean with syllabi-tailored quality learning materials and tuition in a Post-COVID world. With great excitement, she brought the projects to her superiors, but they did not share our excitement. She was almost more disappointed than I was.

I shared some of these lows not because I feel particularly transparent in this season of my life, but to make it clear that I know and understand all too well what it feels like to have a massive dream against the backdrop of a world that doesn't seem to see, hear or understand you. I know what it is to be mad at the world because it seems like there is insufficient help to see your dreams and visions to their end. I've been in pit-like situations more times than I care to count, and almost every time, I've met someone who wanted to rescue me from the mockery and difficulty which came as unwelcome companions to the guest of my dreams. Each time my rescuer's intent was well placed, but his or her ability to realize that intent was always just a little too late to prevent me from making the trek to Egypt.

These are defining moments. The help that could save you from the pit will not come in time only because you must make the trek to Egypt. After all, Egypt is where you will rise.

YOU WILL BE UNDERVALUED

20 pieces of silver.

This man who would save hundreds of thousands, possibly millions of people, from starvation was sold for a mere 20 pieces of silver.

This man, who would become overseer to the world's most thriving economy, was sold for a mere 20 pieces of silver.

20 pieces of silver.

When I read this bit of intel, I instinctively knew that this value was unfathomably lower than what Joseph was actually worth. After all, it was less than the 30 pieces of silver that Judas was paid in exchange for his betrayal of Jesus. Still, I wanted to contextualize this in a way that would make it tangible to those of our time. So I embarked on a mission to discover what 20 pieces of silver would be worth today. After days and hours of research with very little to show for it, I called on external help.

My friend, Dennis[10], shared this:

"Let's use Matthew 26:15 as an anchor point to help answer this question.

---

[10] Dennis Adams is both a theologue and an Organizational Development and Change Strategist. Dennis has a BA in Pastoral Studies from the West Indies School of Theology and an MSc. in Organizational Leadership from CUNY-Lehman College. Dennis is also the founder and chief curator of NowProclaim.com, a space for voicing and dissecting the contemporary, Caribbean, Christian perspective while also serving as a home for theological resources and works that represent the shifting landscape and thought of the church within his eastern Caribbean cultural context.

Archibald Robertson (1930) estimates that thirty silver shekels were equal to 120 denarii, less than five English pounds, less than twenty-five dollars ($25), the price of a slave's life. (NB. There was no doubt that contempt for Jesus was in the minds of both the Sanhedrin and Judas in this bargain.)

According to John Wesley (1765) thirty pieces of silver was about three pounds fifteen shillings sterling; or sixteen dollars sixty seven cents, this was also the price of a slave during the period surrounding Exodus 21:32. John Gill (1746) also agrees that 30 pieces of Silver would equate to "three pounds fifteen shillings."

Marvin Vincent (2013) actually argues that the 30 shekels mentioned in Matthew (which in itself was a reference to Zechariah 11:12) were shekels of the sanctuary, of standard weight, and therefore heavier than the ordinary shekel. Vincent (2013) reckons the Jerusalem shekel at seventy-two cents, the sum would be twenty-one dollars and sixty cents. He argues that that was also the price which, by the Mosaic law, a man was condemned to pay if his ox should gore a servant (Exo 21:32). So you have a value that ranges from $17.67 to $21.61. This would put your 20 shekels at 2/3 this value, which would be $11.78 to $14.40... or 2/3 of a Slave or 2/3 or the Potter's Field.

Essentially, Joseph was valued at 2/3 a slave. Not even a whole slave. And this, in its own way, is quite instructive.

The reality is that when we find ourselves at the place of empty cisterns, human beings lose both the desire and the capacity to measure us accurately.

At that low point, no one sees how beautiful or handsome you are.

At that low point, no one sees how much of a great overseer you are.

At that low point, most people forget how you saved your team from complete annihilation by scoring an almost impossible goal.

At that low point, no one sees how gifted you are.

At that low point, all they are concerned with is how they can get the best deal for you – the best out of you for the lowest price possible – and in doing so, they will have zero qualms about undervaluing or devaluing you.

Be not surprised that you, whose destiny is to stand before kings and queens and impart wisdom that will multiply their wealth, will be ignored when giving valuable suggestions at your work meetings.

Be not surprised that you, whose destiny it is to mother legions of children, will be looked down upon because you are unable to birth children.

Be not surprised that you, whose destiny is to go gold, diamond, or platinum, are told your voice is too nasal, too soft, or not what they're looking for right now.

Be not surprised, for in empty cisterns, you will be undervalued.

That is a promise.

YOUR COAT OF MANY COLORS WILL BE TORN

23 So when Joseph arrived, his brothers ripped off the beautiful robe he was wearing

—

Genesis 37:23

The very first thing his brothers did in the commission of their act of evil toward him was to rid Joseph of the coat of many colors that symbolized his father's favor as well as all of the things that he was going to become; a man of authority, regality and wealth. In tearing the robe, his brothers ensured that the traders who would come to purchase Joseph were robbed of any indication that this young man whom they would purchase for only 20 pieces of silver was once clad in a robe befitting royalty. In our personal lives, the loss of the robe here can be instructive to our journey in a multitude of ways, but I will focus on two.

The first lesson here is to know that losing material things doesn't mean that you've lost the gifts that God has placed within you.

Along this journey, there will be instances where we lose valuable, tangible things; things that in our society are symbolic of what place we should occupy in this world – money, cars, clothes, jewelry – but they do not constitute a loss of the most precious of our things: our calling, gifting, and talents.

The second lesson here is to know that you can recover after a loss because you carry God-given gifts and abilities.

Joseph's robe was maliciously stripped off him and torn, but because Joseph still had the gifts of leadership, management, and interpreting dreams, he was able to recover multiple times during his experience in Egypt. When he landed in Potiphar's house, it was his astute management and diligence towards his assignments that resulted in Potiphar giving him full charge of his house. When he landed in prison, it was his strategic positioning as overseer of the prison that resulted in the butler and the baker being assigned to him. Likewise, when you go through difficult seasons – empty cisterns – remember that God has placed within you everything you need to recover in the next phases of your life.

SOME WILL THINK THAT YOU ARE LOST

Then the brothers killed a young goat and dipped Joseph's robe in its blood. 32 They sent the beautiful robe to their father with this message: "Look at what we found. Doesn't this robe belong to your son?" 33 Their father recognized it immediately. "Yes," he said, "it is my son's robe. A wild animal must have eaten him. Joseph has clearly been torn to pieces!" 34 Then Jacob tore his clothes and dressed himself in burlap. He mourned deeply for his son for a long time. 35 His family all tried to comfort him, but he refused to be comforted. "I will go to my grave[e] mourning for my son," he would say, and then he would weep. 36 Meanwhile, the Midianite traders[f] arrived in Egypt, where they sold Joseph to Potiphar, an officer of Pharaoh, the king of Egypt. Potiphar was captain of the palace guard.

–

Genesis 29: 19-20 (NLT)

The season of empty cisterns was a period of significant loss for Joseph. He was treated in the most undignified and disrespectful manner, lost his coat of many colors, and would come to lose his home and family.

After selling him to Egyptian traders, Joseph's brothers concocted an elaborate story to present to their father as an explanation for the disappearance of his most beloved son. They would dip the young man's coat of many colors in goat's blood. They would send it to their father, along with a message that his faithful, most favored son had been killed by a wild animal. They would tell their father that his prized son had been torn to pieces. This plan, devious in every way, and Jacob's ensuing reaction, stood out to me in a way they had not before.

Along the journey to fulfilling purpose, some of us have elicited or will elicit from our grandparents, parents, aunts, uncles, friends, siblings, and cousins the deep mourning of a life lost while we are still very much alive; still with breath. And I do not speak only of the mourning elicited when a child goes down a dubious road. I also speak of the mourning elicited when a child – a grandson, granddaughter, niece, nephew, cousin or sibling – has seemingly been stripped of all of their once evident potential.

This child who once sang beautifully, has lost his/her voice. This woman who was once so vibrant, had lost her luster. This child who once was so sure that he/she would become the nation's Prime Minister, has lost his/her vision and passion. The promising athlete has torn his ACL and is swimming in a pool of depression. And so, like Jacob, they grieve. Deeply.

On your end, this is the juncture of the journey where you may feel without the support of the people or person dearest to you. It is a tangible withdrawal of their presence, kindness, and support. It may not be the fruit of deep antagonism, nor may it be a conscious withdrawal on their part, but you will very likely feel alone at this juncture in the season. For Joseph, that lack of support was the cause of a logistical reality, but for you, it may simply be an existential reality. Some people dear to you may no longer be able to see you, and inadvertently they may no longer be able to see the things you dreamt and spoke of. But as with many things, it is only for a time.

Nearing the end of Joseph's story, we are told that Jacob is informed that the son he believed was dead is alive, and he is transported to Egypt to see him function at the height of all of his promise. In the same way, many who believe that you are lost – who have been unable to see you during this season of your life – will be carried to a place in the future where they will find out that what they have believed about you is far from the truth. They will find out that you are alive, doing well, and prospering in the places where God has placed you.

teased.

19 Potiphar was furious when he heard his wife's story about how Joseph had treated her. 20 So he took Joseph and threw him into the prison where the king's prisoners were held, and there he remained.

–

Genesis 29: 19-20 (NLT)

In October 2018, I returned to Saint Lucia after having spent six weeks in Detroit, San Diego, and Washington DC as part of a US Department of State-sponsored program called the Young Leaders of the Americas Initiative. I would return, extremely tired, to a disgruntled Sixth Form class. My growing awareness that teaching wasn't where I wanted or needed to be in that particular season of my life transitioned to a blaring one.

I had had a difficult summer filled with anxiety, weight loss, and panic attacks. The pressures to which I returned were slowly guiding me back into that zone, so with no emergency fund and some debt still in tow, I dropped off my letter of resignation. I would leave at the end of the Christmas term.

The plan was to fly to New York to spend time with family, sleep a ton, and immerse myself in Christian ministry to clear my head.

Oh, wait. I didn't tell you about the investor who contacted me on LinkedIn and promised to bankroll Wakonté?

No worries. I've mentioned it in a previous chapter, but you'll hear about it in greater detail later in this Chapter.

That's a sure thing. But back to this …

Some of the most devastating moments in my journey can be described as "teases". In these moments, I felt like I was on the verge of success. I felt like I was on the verge of walking into so many of the things that I had dreamed of, but out of the blue, something would come up and throw a wrench into things. Sometimes these wrenches looked like delays, and other times they looked and felt like outright losses. You've probably felt or experienced them too. It's that juncture of the journey called "teased".

"Teased" is where you come out of empty cisterns and begin to function in a space that is more suited or aligned with your God-given gifts. It is also more reflective of your dream. In this space, there are semblances of success. In this space, you are rising, and your place of service looks more like where you should be and what you should be doing. Honor it. Relish it. Work hard at it. But don't get too comfortable because it's not the real thing.

Joseph didn't know it then, but because of the gift of hindsight, we know that his experience of rising in Potiphar's household was merely a tease of what would eventually come; a miniature replica of what would become his final destination. Joseph's season in Potiphar's house is what I like to call...

AN ALMOST MANIFESTATION

One would think that someone who entered a foreign land as a slave would experience the height of difficulty in rebranding themselves as anything other than, and if they were able to rebrand themselves, they would need significant blocks of time to do so. But this was not so with Joseph. Joseph quickly ascended to the heights of power in Potiphar's house, and he knew it. He said as much when he told Potiphar's wife, *"With me in charge, my master does not concern himself with anything in the house; everything he owns he has entrusted to my care. No one is greater in this house than I am. My master has withheld nothing from me except you, because you are his wife."*

There are points in your journey where you will experience a success that so wildly contrasts the season of empty cisterns that you will be tempted to believe that you are near the destination of your dreams. But it is not the real thing. As a matter of fact, it is a miniature version of the real thing. Look at it like this: Potiphar's Household? Minute when compared to the Egyptian nation.

So I was telling you about the big-time investor who promised to bankroll Wakonté. He connected with me on LinkedIn, and after numerous conversations, I felt that he had gotten the vision; he understood the mission. I felt like he had grasped firmly the value of what I was doing. For me, that was a big deal, particularly because on this journey, I had adopted a posture of hesitancy when it came to taking investors' money.

Anyhoo, our conversations progressed to the point that we decided to meet up in New York to fine-tune the details of our arrangement. I would be given a monthly salary, more money than I had ever made, and access to his nice, cushy office in a well-known building in Manhattan in exchange for me being a program developer for his budding media company. I just knew that I had come to the point where my hopes and dreams of creating a storytelling empire would be realized. And it fit in perfectly with my plans to quit teaching, so even without a contract in hand[11], I confidently landed in New York. With approximately $300USD to my name.

Based on the subheading under which this story falls, you should know by now that my big investment never materialized. But let me tell you more.

Mr. Hotshot Investor landed in New York approximately three weeks after I'd arrived. We met at his nice, cushy office in that very well-known building in Manhattan to talk

---

[11]I promise. I know about the value of contracts. I promise, I know about the value of getting things in writing. However, I felt so convinced that this was an opportunity that was going to change my life that I was content to just land in New York with hope and positive expectations.

business, after which we went to dinner accompanied by his Chief Technology Officer and another one of his acquaintances.

From our meeting in that office, I was in a state of deep unease. I knew I was in deep doo-doo. At the meeting, he explained to me that he had found himself in a predicament. He was in the midst of an acquisition for which he thought he'd secured the financing, but at the last minute, his financiers pulled out. He didn't say it outright, but his need to share with me the details of the predicament was, in a way, saying to me, "Hey, that thing we talked about? The reason you're in New York with $300 dollars to your name? It's not going to happen."

At dinner, I knew I was in even deeper doo-doo than I initially thought. He paid for dinner, and the card was declined. Mon Dieu. He eventually produced a card that was good to go. But in that moment, it became clear to me that unless some sort of miracle happened that I wasn't going to be able to capitalize on that opportunity. This "almost" manifestation was a no-go.

In the end, I stayed in New York for a few months after our meeting. During that time, I worked toward helping him raise the necessary capital to make his acquisition a reality while picking up freelance web design and development jobs to strengthen my very, very weak bank account. In

New York, at that. He made the acquisition by the skin of his teeth, and a few months later, I was flying home to spend some final moments with my dying grandmother. The investor, to this day, has never said, "I can't meet the terms of our verbal agreement", and has never again brought it up. I was this [pinch your finger with barely a hair in between] close, but it was not to be, for I would be going to prison.

But before I land there, please take the following notes…

BE WILLING TO SERVE IN SMALLER PLACES

Dreams are massive, and while they may be given overnight, they manifest over time. This is lost on many of us. We function in a fast-paced, microwave-driven world so we want what we saw in those dreams NOW, often turning down our noses at smaller places or opportunities. But be open to serving in smaller places.

Joseph's willingness to serve in smaller places is evident throughout the depth and breadth of his story, and it was his attitude while serving in these smaller places that eventually made room for him to become second-in-command in Egypt. Each time he encountered the catalyst to the next leg of his journey, he was on assignment, serving with diligence and excellence in places remarkably smaller than he saw in his dreams. This is an attitude and posture worthy of emulation.

You've had dreams of rule, power, and reign, but be open to serving in smaller places.

You've had dreams of playing in the highest, most recognized professional league but treat your community league with the same dedication and respect as you would the big leagues.

You've had dreams of preaching to millions, but treat the audience of three with the dignity and respect that you would treat the thousands.

You've had dreams of closing 6-figure contracts but treat the the client with the 4-figure contract with the same enthusiasm and respect that you would treat the 6 figure contract.

You've had dreams of being the top dog with the office with the view, but treat the cubicle respectfully.

You've had dreams big dreams but small steps will take you to destination.

Be willing to serve in smaller spaces.

& BE WILLING TO LEAVE YOUR ROBE

But he refused. "With me in charge," he told her, "my master does not concern himself with anything in the house; everything he owns he has entrusted to my care. 9No one is greater in this house than I am. My master has withheld nothing from me except you, because you are his wife. How then could I do such a wicked thing and sin against God?" 10And though she spoke to Joseph day after day, he refused to go to bed with her or even be with her. 11 One day he went into the house to attend to his duties, and none of the household servants was inside. 12 She caught him by his cloak and said, "Come to bed with me!" But he left his cloak in her hand and ran out of the house.

-

Genesis 39: 8-12 (NLT)

When I got to this part of the story, I was like, "What is up with Joseph and these robes and coats and cloaks?" These garments – the ones symbolic of the promise of regality, wealth, authority, and prestige – were always featured when he found himself in any sort of trouble. This time was no different.

Joseph was "coming up in life". The man who purchased him after his brothers' betrayal had eyes to see the gift of management he possessed. What he saw led him to give Joseph charge over all of his affairs. And Joseph was so, so good at his job. He was so good that if he were a young entrepreneur in 2023, he'd probably have been posted in Forbes 30 Under 30 or given some other profligate title. The young man was coming up, but he would not long find himself in a situation that would pull the rug from under him and take him back to square one.

Based on Biblical descriptions, Joseph was exceedingly handsome. That man was finer than the lead in a push-point pencil. Not only was his face great to look at, but he also had a great body. And Potiphar's wife wasn't blind. So she saw. And she wanted what she saw. And she was determined to have what she wanted. At any cost. However, she had a stumbling block to fulfilling her desires.

Joseph respected Potiphar deeply, and he feared God even more. He wanted absolutely no part of her debauchery, so he refused Madame Potiphar's advances. More than once. Consistently. Each time he rejected her, she persisted, growing more assertive in the pursuit and nature of her advances until that fateful day when her desires could no longer withstand Joseph's denials. She grabbed him by his cloak. He left it in her hands and fled.

How many people do you know who would have been closer to their dreams if they had decided to throw integrity out the window?

I know many entrepreneurs, myself included, who would have gotten the funding they desired if they had embellished their stories only a little bit or fallen prey to the pressure to make wild forecasts that held high probabilities of not being true. These people have suffered a little more for doing the right thing. Their journeys have been extended, and some of them are stuck. On the other hand, there are those so fastly attached to the dreams they've beheld that they are often willing to do almost anything to get to the destination. More often than not, their actions end up doing more harm than good to themselves, their families, and their communities.

And please, don't restrict your perception of compromise to the more apparent violations like using our bodies and sex perversely, stealing, or lying. Sometimes compromise is marked by forsaking God-given duties to family and friends. Some have left their parents to wither away without care in their old age because they gave their dreams greater prominence than duty. Sometimes compromise is marked by going back on one's word; cutting out business partners from deals even when they've met their end of the bargain.

When your integrity is tested – it will be – always be willing to leave your cloak. Do not be so fastly attached to a foreshadowing of the real thing. Do not be so attached to the comforts of Potiphar's house that you forsake wise, good, and honorable paths. It is but a miniature version of the actual dream that you've beheld. It is but an "almost" manifestation".

Leave the robe. Even when it means going to prison.

prison.

19 Potiphar was furious when he heard his wife's story about how Joseph had treated her. 20 So he took Joseph and threw him into the prison where the king's prisoners were held, and there he remained.

–

Genesis 29: 19-20 (NLT)

With our Jansport bags on our backs, we marched out of our fourth form classroom, singing fervently, and harmoniously, "Prison ah nuh bed a roses". Our impassioned chorus may have deceived listeners into believing that we had personally endured the harsh realities of a steel-barred room, but we'd only ever encountered the mild form: school.

To us, the reality of prison was distant; inconceivable. In our minds, we were only singing a popular song and would never really know what prison truly felt like. But for those of us who carried our dreams and the hopes of others, we were only fooling ourselves, for we would, in reality, encounter prison. We would learn firsthand the truth of our refrain: "Prison ah 'nuh bed a roses".

Likewise, if you carry your dreams and the hopes of others, like many of us who walked out of that fourth-form classroom, you will encounter or have encountered prison. But don't take my word for it. Take the litmus test.

Stuck.

Everyone seems to be moving forward except you.

Progress is seemingly averse to you.

And what's worse?

You're here because you did the right thing.

You helped people.

You carried yourself with integrity.

You opted not to lie.

You opted not to steal.

You opted not to grant sexual favors to your boss for the sake of a promotion.

You did all of the right things, but you are here.

Stuck.

Alone with your thoughts.

Not moving.

Stagnant.

Living life on other people's terms.

Stuck.

Waiting.

Stuck.

Waiting.

Sounds or feels familiar?

Welcome to prison.

But before we check you in, there is something you should be aware of on this leg of your journey.

GOD IS WITH YOU

21But the Lord was with Joseph in the prison and showed him his faithful love. And the Lord made Joseph a favorite with the prison warden. 22Before long, the warden put Joseph in charge of all the other prisoners and over everything that happened in the prison. 23The warden had no more worries, because Joseph took care of everything. The Lord was with him and caused everything he did to succeed.

—

Genesis 39: 21-23 (NLT)

It's been a wild ride, and you're here. You've been thrown into an empty cistern, undervalued and sold into slavery, teased with the fulfillment of the promise, and thrown into prison for doing the right thing. At this point of the journey, you're probably asking, hopelessly, "Where is God?"

At this juncture, it is understandable that we are tempted to think that God is nowhere in the picture. We think He is not near us. He has left us. He has forsaken us. However, these thoughts do not match the truth, for just as God was with Joseph, so He is with us.

God was with Joseph from the genesis of his life, blessing him with gifts and abilities. God was with him in the pit, making intervention and saving his life, God was with him in Potiphar's house, and God was with him in prison.

When you are going through difficulties, and life has brought you to a place where you feel stuck, remember that God is with you. He has blessed you with gifts and abilities, and he has made salvatory intervention in the moments where you believed that death would be your portion. It is uncharacteristic of him to leave you, forsake you or abandon you. As a matter of fact, it is because he is with you...

YOU WILL EXPERIENCE FAVOR

Without question, Joseph had a tumultuous journey, but there's something that stuck out to me. It didn't matter where Joseph found himself, he experienced favor. This may seem strange to some reading this, because favor is usually identified as something evident only at one's highest points. However, Joseph's life is evidence that we can also experience favor at our lowest points. Even in prison. In other words, favor does not depart from us simply because we are stuck. This in mind…

DON'T FIGHT IT. HONE YOUR CRAFT.

Prison is designed in such a way that it limits your movement and forces on you a monotonous existence. It is likely that your primary instinct will be to try to find yourself out of the cage. But prison is not something that you can claw your way out of through sheer determination. You are going to need a skilled advocate or convincing witness to speak up on your behalf. Thus, after the sentence has been handed down? Don't fight it.

So what do we do here?

Don't give in to feelings like boredom and despair.

So…

What do we do?

Joseph did something instructive to all of our journeys. Despite being in a place that he didn't deserve to be, he found ways to use his imprisonment as an opportunity to hone his gifts of management and dream interpretation.

During this season, you should do the same. Use this time of stuck to hone your gifts and abilities.

Keep practicing the piano, guitar, or drums. Keep training your voice. Keep writing, even though you ball up 100s of sheets of paper and throw them in the bin after. Learn that new language. Keep producing even though you feel eons away from the genius you'd like to become.

Personally, I haven't always done this part well. As I write this, I've twisted myself into a pretzel about how slowly my life is moving. I also left writing to go out to brainstorm my next 6 business ideas, and I even started one too. In the end, I was able to recenter myself and come back to finish what I hope will be a tremendous blessing to you who are reading. I shared the experience to say, that piling up certificates, taking courses, or doing things that you cannot clearly tie to an immediate outcome or the manifestation of your dream can be frustrating, but keep at it because all of that hard work will pay off many, many seasons down the line. When you least expect it.

This brings us to the next point…

So this man – this man here being Joseph – was stuck, and the prison guard decided to leave full run of the prison to him almost as if to say, "You're going nowhere, paddy, so might as well handle this". What's more is that he even assigned specific people to Joseph. But it was not without purpose, because in order for Joseph to move to the next stage of his journey, he would have to…

INTERPRET THE DREAMS OF OTHERS

You are in the fight of your life. You're trying to make sense of why you're in a place you probably shouldn't be. You're stuck, nothing is going your way, and your desire is to focus your energy on how you're going to get out of this place of shackles. You are broke; you are nowhere near the level of financial freedom or career fulfillment that you had dreamed of having at this stage of your life. Understandably, you'd like to focus on chasing the bag, and sometimes chasing the bag requires an ultra focus on personal goals and plans. However, they just won't leave you alone.

A talented young man in your youth group needs some money to purchase a camera, and another straight A student needs some assistance with purchasing his school books. Someone is asking you to give away 10 hours monthly to mentor a group of young people who are in tremendous need when you only just decided that you are putting a price tag on every hour of your time. What is going on?

It is understandable that the thing that you are least likely interested in doing while in prison is focusing on the goals and aspirations of others. You're not upset that they have goals. Hell, you're even happy to be a silent cheerleader. But putting in the time, effort, and sometimes money to help them attain their goals while you're struggling with yours? Na, man. It goes against the most basal human instinct of self-preservation.

But here's what will to happen to you: People will be assigned you in this season of your life. Your job will be to help them bring their visions into spheres of clarity, understanding, and practicality. It can be through the use of your finances, it can be through the dispatch of your wisdom and life experience, and it can also be through the use of your gifts. You won't have to look for these assignments. They will be in prison, just like you, and they will be assigned to you.

Some time later, Pharaoh's chief cup-bearer and chief baker offended their royal master. 2Pharaoh became angry with these two officials, 3 and he put them in the prison where Joseph was, in the palace of the captain of the guard. 4 They remained in prison for quite some time, and the captain of the guard assigned them to Joseph, who looked after them. 5 While they were in prison, Pharaoh's cup-bearer and baker each had a dream one night, and each dream had its own meaning. 6 When Joseph saw them the next morning, he noticed that they both looked upset. 7 "Why do you look so worried today?" he asked them. 8 And they replied,

"We both had dreams last night, but no one can tell us what they mean.""Interpreting dreams is God's business," Joseph replied. "Go ahead and tell me your dreams."

—

Genesis 40:1-8 (NLT)

You will meet people who are stuck on their journeys to purpose fulfilled. You will meet people trying to make sense of the dreams placed on their hearts and minds, and your job will be to help them. If I didn't make it clear enough in the previous paragraphs, allow me to elucidate: Prison will demand that you help others interpret their dreams, and what you do here is crucial to your destiny because it is someone whose dreams you helped along who will mention you to Pharaoh.

But…

There's a but.

From my personal life, I've observed that I have a tendency to embrace the mandate of helping others interpret their dreams a little too well. And this may prove true for you also. Until recently, I found myself looking to assist in interpreting the dreams of even those not assigned to me. It left me burnt out and unable to devote what should primarily be a season of isolation, thinking, pruning, and honing to anything else but the interpretation of the dreams of others. As I write this book, I am reminded that the mandate here is not to assist in interpreting the dreams of everyone but to assist in interpreting the dreams of those assigned to me. Likewise, in this season be mindful that your mandate here is not to interpret the dreams of everyone whose paths cross yours. The mandate is to interpret the dreams of those assigned to you.

And yes, it may often feel like…

EVERYONE IS PROGRESSING. EXCEPT YOU

At least it seems so.

Both the butler and the baker came into prison when Joseph was already there. He helped them interpret their dreams, and they both left prison. Before him.

Have you ever taught someone how to play an instrument, make beautiful items out of wood or stone, wire a house, get the best out of their entry-level camera, or do anything? You invested time and energy for years honing your skill or craft. You're good at it. As a matter of fact, you're excellent, and so your next thing is to pass on that knowledge/ expertise to a mentee/apprentice. After a few months of sharing your knowledge, your student is called and given a massive offer to do a massive job that you, in all your years of dedication to the craft, have never been offered. At the end of the day, you are happy that your student is progressing, and you celebrate their wins (you really should). Nevertheless, your natural instinct as a human being is to try to figure out what you're doing wrong; to ask, "God, when?".

The answer to your question is that it will happen at the right time.

Do not worry when people you trained and mentored in the workplace are given promotions while you remain in the same position. It's not a competition, anyways.

Do not worry when people who made entry into your field/discipline well after you are given awards and recognized while you remain in the background.

Do not worry.

You are exactly where you should be. Take this time to live unhurried, think, grow, and rest, because there will come a season where the measure of responsibility that will be placed upon your shoulders will be so great that it will leave no room for these unhurried moments.

Do not worry. As a matter of fact, be like Joseph and welcome the ascension/release of others over yours. View it as a strategic occurrence that will work in your favor.

After Joseph had interpreted the baker's and the cup-bearer's dreams, he knew with immediacy that their releases were impending and would likely take place before his. However, he didn't cop an attitude because they, whose dreams he had interpreted, would be released from prison. Before him. No. Instead, Joseph being owner of divine wisdom and a highly strategic nature, saw this as an opportunity to…

ASK FOR A FAVOR

Perhaps you have been raised in an environment or cultural milieu markedly different from mine, and you have 0 problems asking for what you want. But where I'm from? Asking for the things you want, especially if what you want is help, can oftentimes be a bad look. It's a pride thing. It's a shame thing. It's a very puzzling construct. You're *big* and should have this covered. You shouldn't need help. You shouldn't need others. **Self-sufficiency & Independence** is the name of the game.

And please remember me and do me a favor when things go well for you. Mention me to Pharaoh, so he might let me out of this place.

–

Genesis 39: 21-23 (NLT)

There is also the Christian "ideal" that one does things for another, expecting nothing in return. Thus, if you help someone, you shouldn't ask them for anything in return. Premised on the things I've shared here, it should therefore be no surprise that when I read Joseph asking the cup-bearer to remember him, I was a little taken aback. I was like "Whoa!" Joseph, a stalwart of faith and reliance on God, is asking another human being for a favor? However, looking at it without my cultural lens, I recognize that this act embodies Joseph's strategic nature and highlights the importance of being both mindful and "opportunistic".

Joseph didn't request favors from everyone he had helped, demonstrating his discerning approach. He asked a specific individual. He asked no favor of the baker, likely due to the foreboding nature of the baker's dream. Instead, he asked the cup-bearer. Because of the nature of the cup-bearer's dream, Joseph was very well aware that the cup-bearer would be released not far off, and he would eventually have Pharaoh's ear. Joseph was swift to capitalize on that bit of knowledge. He assumed no posture of feigned humility. He assumed no posture of vain pride. He simply and courageously asked for a favor.

In our own lives, it's essential to recognize that not everyone we help will be in a position to return the favor. Still, when the right opportunity presents itself, it is okay to ask for a favor.

Don't be afraid to ask.

release.

Pharaoh sent for Joseph at once, and he was quickly brought from the prison. After he shaved and changed his clothes, he went in and stood before Pharaoh. .

—

Genesis 41:14 (NLT)

"Ms. Swaggerific".

This was my nickname during my stay at the Sir Arthur Lewis Hall of Residence (SAL Hall) on Saint John's Road, St. Augustine.

"Star gyal".

That was my other nickname, often heard when I traversed the paved paths at the UWI, St. Augustine.

They weren't without basis.

If you met me between the ages of, say 19 and 21, you would have met an über confident woman; a woman so sure that her final destination was success and great things that it manifested in a distinct swagger. And yeah, I was nice with it too.

I liked wearing nice clothes, nice watches, and particular brand names. Now, I was in fact a student, so I wasn't wearing Rolexes or *'nun* but I did have a couple of nice timepieces from Anne Klein and Michael Kors. You also wouldn't catch me dead without a pair of RayBan Aviators, my long-sleeved shirts and suits were tailored and monogrammed and I had three signature leather jackets in black, brown and off-white. If I may say so again, your girl was nice with it. I had a capsule wardrobe long before I even knew what they were, and I was exuding "quiet luxury" in perhaps a not so quiet way. I was clean, I was exceedingly smooth and I had a distinct vibe.

By my 23rd or 24th year of life, I had morphed into an entirely different creature. To help put into perspective how great of a metamorphosis it was, consider that I've always been one of the more understated women in my family when it came to *dressing up*. Even in my smooth era. This new era of understatement was so bad that my mother, aunts, sister and sometimes cousins would be stuck as to why I wasn't doing more and would often silently question me with their eyes. Occasionally, they would buy me new clothes, etc, and I really wasn't having it. I would tell them to give me the money instead; I had alternate uses for the cash. I just didn't care enough to keep up an image.

I was flailing at life. Nothing appeared to be going right, even though I worked insane hours trying to build a design and marketing agency. I was paying off some unexpected student debt, which nearly took me to my grave. Sidenote: I hate debt and I'm never doing it again. Not in this lifetime. The bank had zero mercy. But yes, I was completely over it. And it showed in how little attention I paid to my outward appearance. I had been stripped of my "coat of many colors".

Fast forward to today, and I wouldn't say that I'm out of prison just yet, so I've, for the most part, kept my "prison" clothes. I remain very understated, and if I was a dude, I'd probably be carrying an ungroomed beard until my season/moment of release. However, I sense that my release is near, because in my own way, and at my own pace, I am ready to or getting ready to...

SHAVE AND CHANGE CLOTHES

Beards cover one's face. They make one less visible; less identifiable and stand as the antithesis of transparency. Biblically, they have also been indications of the suffering of a man. These things considered, Joseph's beard was indeed a fitting look for his season of obscurity. However, he did something worthy of emulation when he was released into service. He shaved and changed his clothes.

The transformation of Joseph's attire carries a significance that cannot be dismissed as mere happenstance. Biblical scholars have delved deeply into the possible motivations behind his decision to shave and change his clothes. Among the numerous theories, one particularly compelling explanation suggests that Joseph was eager to assimilate into Egyptian culture and stay en vogue with contemporary fashion. Joseph's adaptability shines through this narrative, painting the portrait of a man who remains flexible and agile, perpetually in sync with the changing times and seasons.

His foresight is evident in his every move, including his carefully chosen attire – a testament to his strategic mindset. Furthermore, Joseph's actions exemplify a keen awareness that different environments often necessitate different garments. Ultimately, his willingness to cast off the vestments of one season and eagerly embrace those of another only serves to underscore Joseph's readiness for growth and evolution throughout his journey to fulfilled dreams.

You, likewise, in your season of release, will need to emulate a similar form of adaptability and discernment. In your season of release, there will be a need for you to be able to switch things up, and to determine what mindsets, attitudes and even garments will work for where God is taking you. If there is a need for it, do not hesitate to shave and change your clothes.

MOVE CONFIDENTLY

Confidence was something that Joseph never seemed to lack, and it was probably because his confidence stemmed from his knowledge and belief in a God who is omnipotent, omniscient, and omnipresent. But for some of us, particularly those of us who come from cultures that teach flawed conceptualizations of humility, there are lessons to be taken here.

Confidence is humility because confidence facilitates a full expression of the gifts and powers that God has placed within you. Confidence reveals God's glory, through you, to men. And the truth is that humility will never call for you to hamper or hide the gifts and abilities that God has placed within you because it hides God's glory; it takes from it. And that is, in fact, the definition of pride.

Be like Joseph. Move confidently. Let it be a boast

Joseph confidently told Pharaoh the meaning of his dreams, and he confidently told him how he should navigate the impending seasons. In so doing, Joseph revealed to the Egyptian Pharaoh a God who is all-knowing, precise, merciful, and wise. Likewise, in the full expression of your gifts and talents, there should be a revelation of God's majesty, splendor, and character. Even when it makes others uncomfortable, walk in it.

Move confidently. Also…

OVER DELIVER

Joseph's interpretations carried with them an element that perhaps Pharaoh didn't expect of him. He was brought in simply to tell Pharaoh what his dreams meant. He could have said, "You will have 7 years of abundance followed by 7 years of famine," and be done. However, in typical Joseph fashion, he went the extra mile. After he shared the meaning of Pharaoh's dreams, without being asked, he took the lead and offered solutions. He told Pharaoh what he should do both during the seasons of abundance and seasons of famine prophesied in his dreams. Joseph over-delivered in his place of service, and that over-delivery brought him one step closer to realizing his dreams.

As someone who has experienced abuse in the corporate space, I remain largely averse to corporations taking advantage of employees. It is, therefore, no surprise that over-delivery when helping the powerful bring their dreams to life is difficult for me to advocate. However, the reality remains that you and I will find ourselves in certain places that will demand that we demonstrate our value to key stakeholders; employers, investors, ministers of government, or church leaders. These places will often be tied to continuances or extensions of our freedom, and our best bet is always to over-deliver.

cross &...

19 Potiphar was furious when he heard his wife's story about how Joseph had treated her. 20 So he took Joseph and threw him into the prison where the king's prisoners were held, and there he remained.

—

Genesis 29: 19-20 (NLT)

A few years ago, I came across a podcast hosted by one Dr. Tim Mackie: "Understanding My Strange Bible". This podcast would come to play an influential role in helping me see certain portions of Scripture in a new light. Ultimately, it would make sharing the gospel an intimate part of everything I would write. In this podcast, every, *single* episode, Dr. Mackie, would find some way to guide his listeners to the power of the gospel. No matter what book he was preaching from. As I sat to write this book, I wondered how I could do the same.

As a Christian, I felt deeply that there was more to Joseph's story – a more which transcended even the lessons that I had already taken – and so I began to ask questions of the text.

How should this story influence my theology of work and purpose?

What does this story tell me about dreams and how they ought to be viewed in the broader context of my Christianity?

What about Joseph's story could lead us to Calvary?

What about his travail could remind us of our wretched state and Christ's sacrifice?

It took a couple of weeks before I would fully understand it. It took me reading the Chapters over and over, and mulling on them day after day before it would make any bit of sense to me. I went through the vagaries of life, each day, and one day it popped up in my spirit. Boom!

THE DREAM IS THE CROSS

When does this end?

I know, I know.

Nonetheless, if at this point you find yourself in a place of immense frustration and fatigue, then this book has done what it has been sent forth to do. It means that you have, to a small extent, experienced, vicariously, the gruel and travails of the journey to fulfilled dreams. It means that you are also at a place where you will better grasp the parallels between the dream and the cross.

This "t"-shaped symbol, the cross, stands at the core of the Christian faith. It is what, to a large extent, differentiates Christianity from other Abrahamic faiths; it is what Christians believe sets Christianity apart as the sole path to follow.

Christians believe that in a broken and hopeless world, God's son, perfect and blameless in all his ways, submitted to the Father's will to pay the ultimate price – a deserving life – so that they could have access to the gift of eternal life. For the Christian, the cross is a symbol of pain, hardship, loneliness, purpose and crucifixion, but most importantly, the cross stands as a symbol of salvation; a gift from the Father and Savior to the saved.

The dream is the cross.

Christians walk, often guided by the belief that one should take up one's cross, and follow Christ; in their doings and sayings, one should seek to serve as a beacon of hope and salvation for others. It also serves as a reference to Simon, who took up the cross in aid of Christ's mission to Calvary. To the Christian, and to even those who are not, the concept of taking up one's cross, or one taking up a cross, is a noble and worthy endeavor. It speaks to sacrifice, self-denial, service, and salvation, values that are seemingly losing their place in 21st. century society. But there is a bright spot. In the midst of this slippage of values, we are in a dispensation where men and women, young and old, are encouraged to pursue their dreams and purpose with all of their might. This is an environment ripe for cultivating lives built on the value of taking up crosses, and one of the ways that one can best fulfill this is by stewarding with diligence the visions/ dreams that God has placed within him/her.

The starting point of stewarding well is recognizing and embracing that we are each…

A TYPE OF CHRIST

This sounds a tad bit like a Messianic complex. But, I promise you, it's not. I was legit as averse to the idea as anyone else. As far as I'm concerned, Jesus paid it all, so why am I a type of Christ? But, please, I beg. Hear me out.

In Christian theology, typology offers a profound exploration of symbolic connections between the Old and New Testaments. It unveils an intricate web of events, people, and statements in the Old Testament as precursors pointing towards Jesus Christ's revelation in the New Testament. Based on the indicators of theological typology, it can be established that Joseph was a type of Christ. Based on the mandate of the Christian faith, you too, are expected to be a type of Christ; a reflection of him and his virtues in the dispensation after his death.

But allow me to make the case for you and I being a type of Christ in like fashion to Joseph.

Joseph endured immense, undeserving pain and toil for the salvation of others. You too, in your journey to fulfilled dreams will endure undeserving pain and toil for the salvation of others.

Even though Joseph's dreams prophesied elevation, accomplishment, and pinnacles, like Christ, he endured whippings [figuratively] and the indignity of being stripped bare on his journey to fulfilled purpose.

He endured the castigation of his family and strangers for the sake of the salvation of others. You too, on your journey to purpose and fulfilled dreams, will endure life's whippings and indignities. You too, on your journey to fulfilled dreams will be stripped bare, and diminished for the sake of the Father. , you too will endure the haters and those who will scorn you for speaking and walking confidently in what God has called you to.

Like Christ, he endured the things which he did while on his Father's business. You too will find yourself in harm's way while on your father's business. And when you do, remember that this is your assignment, and if you sit and rest in God's grace and favor, you will see purpose unfold.

As the parallels between dreams and the cross emerged clearer, it helped me adjust my perspectives around the difficulties I have endured as I trod the journey to purpose fulfilled. As a result, I spend less time trying to escape pits and prisons and more time learning to endure them with grace. I realized that carrying our dreams to their fulfillment is an opportunity to be daily reminded of both Simon's call to assist Christ with the load of the cross and the sacrifice

Christ made for us at Calvary. It is an opportunity to live in submission to the Father's will even on the days where we sweat as blood in Gethsemane; the days where we plead for the cup to be taken from us, if possible. It is an opportunity to emulate one of the most beautiful aspects of the journey to Calvary; carrying heavy, burdensome things for the sake of the salvation of others. And in a sense, yours too.

crown...

41 Pharaoh said to Joseph, "I hereby put you in charge of the entire land of Egypt." 42Then Pharaoh removed his signet ring from his hand and placed it on Joseph's finger. He dressed him in fine linen clothing and hung a gold chain around his neck. 43 Then he had Joseph ride in the chariot reserved for his second-in-command. And wherever Joseph went, the command was shouted, "Kneel down!" So Pharaoh put Joseph in charge of all Egypt. 44 And Pharaoh said to him, "I am Pharaoh, but no one will lift a hand or foot in the entire land of Egypt without your approval."

—

Genesis 41: 41-44 (NLT)

Jacob and eleven of his sons eventually bowed before Joseph. Just like his dream. The vision – its contents inconceivable to his elder brothers – that had visited him in his seventeenth year had manifested. The dream that he had been mocked, scorned, and ridiculed for had come to life. He had toiled to meet its reality. He had suffered for it. And it had come to pass. However, the vibe I get from the passages which capture Joseph's pinnacle is that he probably viewed this manifestation – his father and brothers bowing before him – as pale in comparison to the things he had endured.

He seemed to view that moment of honor as pale in comparison to the feats that he had accomplished. When placed against the difficulties that he had suffered, he seemed to render that moment almost translucent. He had been humiliated, broken, lied on, imprisoned and sometimes forgotten. The idols of safety, comfort, and success if they had existed had been broken. At that moment, it was no more but a sign that he had arrived at the place of the fulfillment of the dream.

Our journeys to purpose fulfilled will be wrought with moments akin to what Joseph had. They will sober us. They will calm us and rip from us the idols of success, reputation, shame, and fear, often masqueraded as wisdom. They will leave us with minimal regard for the vanities of life. They will also leave us crowned and celebrated. You see…

THE CROWN IS RESTITUTION

In Chapter 41 of Genesis, Joseph is elevated after interpreting Pharaoh's dreams and advising him about how he should approach the 14 year span identified in his dream. His elevation was marked by a few actions on Pharaoh's part. Pharaoh placed his personal signet ring on Joseph's finger, he gave to Joseph a new robe made of the finest linen, he put a gold chain around his neck, and he declared him second-in-command

All of the things which Pharaoh gave to Joseph when crowning him, were improved versions of the things he had lost when his brothers had sold him as a slave. His father's gift, the coat of many colors which had been stripped off him and torn, had now been replaced with a new robe of the finest linen. Additionally, he was given a signet ring and a gold chain. His position as his father's favored child and leader amongst his brothers was restituted when he was appointed second only to Pharaoh, but it was also restituted when on his death bed, Jacob gave Joseph an extra portion of the land that he had taken from the Amorites.

You will note that you have come into your season of crowning when many of the things you lost during your time in empty cisterns and prisons are restored to you in equal and extra measure.

In the temporal space, Joseph was winning, but there is something else that stuck out...

THE CROWN IS AS TEMPORAL AS IT IS ETERNAL

Seven chapters after we see Joseph's elevation we are transported to Jacob's deathbed. As in the fashion of the Israelite patriarch, Jacob positions himself to pronounce blessings on each of his sons.

He first calls Joseph into an exclusive meeting where he makes known his death wish, after which he takes/adopts Joseph's two sons as his. Jacob's adoption of Joseph's two sons is his way of bestowing Joseph the rights of the firstborn son: a double portion of his father's inheritance. Thus we see that not only did Joseph's travails result in his crowning in a foreign land, but they also impacted his legacy.

Because of Joseph's faithfulness in a foreign land, his father saw it fit to bypass his elder brothers and place upon him the firstborn's inheritance. Through his sons, Manasseh and Ephraim, long after his body would have withered and returned to dust, his legacy lived on.

When we behold the dream or vision for our lives, oftentimes, our focus is on its temporal end. We see men bowing before us, and we see nice cars, watches, jewelry, or nice homes, but we don't get to see how our characters will be transformed or how our legacies will be carried into the years where our bodies would have left the earth; we place very little significance on what our dreams/visions and how we pursue them mean for our eternal homes. But as is evident in the story of Joseph, our dreams and the manner in which we pursue them have far- reaching impact on our legacies. So...

Walk good.

the final notes.

The previous chapters have fulfilled their mission: to carefully articulate the burden of the dream/cross. They have violently stomped on any ideas that suggest that success happens rapidly or overnight, and they've made clear to dreamers that toil and travail WILL be part of the journey. There are no ifs or buts. As a matter of fact they are requirements of the journey. Even then, because of how they are structured, the Chapters have missed out on a few things. These final notes will capture what couldn't neatly fit into the structured chapters.

NOTE 1: JOSEPH'S DEFICIENCY

There is a tendency for Christians to idealize, idolize and sanitize a Biblical character that has attained significant feats, and without even recognizing it, my admiration of Joseph's resilience in the face of adversity left me in this exact space. I so idealized and sanitized everything that made Joseph him that I did not give due analysis to Joseph's leadership during the famine. Until recently.

Joseph's leadership during the famine ultimately led to the enslavement of the Egyptian people. He kept taking from people in need and, at the end of the day, became an integral part of a greedy gubernatorial superstructure that, without necessity, subjugated the Egyptian people to the loss of everything they owned. Joseph exploited weakness to the point of over-exploitation.

This, in itself, holds a vital lesson for those of us in pursuit of dreams, especially those of us who will function in for-profit or entrepreneurial sectors. It is possible for us to so fervently pursue our giftings and callings to the detriment of others. It therefore speaks to a need to bridle ambitions, to sit in moderation and to know when to stop in our pursuit of material acquisitions.

NOTE 2: EBBS & FLOWS. SLOW. NOT SEAMLESS

Joseph's life was a slow movement; a slow, uneven, lulling rhythm. His dreams and visions came to him as a 17-year-old boy, and not long after, he was sold into slavery in Egypt. He would spend the next 13 years of his life briefly serving in Potiphar's home and the more significant portion in prison.

After Joseph interpreted the cup bearer's dream, it would be an additional two years before his name would be mentioned to Pharaoh, and after his name was mentioned to Pharaoh, it would be an additional 7-10 years before he would see the manifestation of his dreams. Joseph's journey is reflective of the general nature of his life: ebbs and flows; often with more ebbs, but great, great, flows.

His journey was also not seamless. Delving into the narrative of Joseph's life, it initially seems that the various milestones he faced were isolated, one-off incidents that could easily be placed into discrete columns. However, a more studied approach to the story makes it clear that these that Joseph's narrative doesn't unfold in seamless progression. The transitions between stages may not be as sharply delineated as one might initially assume, and in some instances, certain seasons might even appear to echo earlier ones. A prime example of this can be found in the striking parallels shared between Joseph's experiences in the pit and the prison. This perspective encourages us to view our own life journeys in a similar light, recognizing that they are not defined by discrete events but by ever-evolving chapters. If this is grasped well, it gives us the tools to approach our own lives with a richer understanding of the complex tapestry of experiences that will shape us on our journeys to fulfilled dreams.

NOTE 2: CULTIVATE MOMENTS OF JOY

There is a weariness that can take over the soul during the pursuit of the dream. You've seen it. Haters. Pits. Teases. Prisons. Serving. Waiting. Seemingly endless waiting. It is without question a pursuit taxing to mind, body and spirit, and it does not take much for one to stumble upon depression and frustration. For this reason, there ought to be a conscious cultivation of joy. The things happening to you may not necessarily be happy things, but if you can cultivate a mindset that pursues peace in the storm, and contentment with your lot in life, you would have understood how to cultivate moments of joy; you would have discovered that when you rest in God, even in the most dire of situations, you can possess joy.

NOTE 3: IT IS GOD WHO INTERPRETS DREAMS

On more than one occasion, Joseph uttered the words, "It is God who interprets dreams". In other words, "God did it!". It is fitting that the essence of these words should be what the final note in this book is wrapped in.

It is God who interprets dreams. In other words, it is God who determines the unfolding of our dreams, orders our steps, and brings clarity to our paths. It is God who will take every wild stage of this journey and use it for good, even when others – humans and spiritual/supernatural forces – meant for them to harm us.

And this is it!

Perhaps the biggest takeaway from Joseph's sojourn to fulfilled/manifested dreams is that whatever dreams, goals, or plans we have – big or small – it is God who makes them clear and tangible in the realm of reality.

This revelation should empower us to confidently release our hopes and dreams into the hands of the Creator, trusting that he will work all things together for our good.

It is God who interprets dreams.

we give thanks

I must first give props to the Big G: God; my Heavenly Father. My eloquence is pointless here because words simply cannot do you justice. For this I keep it simple and I say, "Thank you, Papa for keeping me, for lifting me, and for working all things together for my good".

I have a family who is unwavering and unrelenting in their support. I am eternally, unwavering, and unrelenting in my gratefulness to them.

To Golda, I'm truly honored that you found the words that I've written worthy enough to *forward*. My life's circumstances have left me with the ability to lock out the voices of others, but in recent times I'm learning that it isn't so much that I don't hear or I'm unaffected by the voices of others, it is a question of whose voice speaks. Truly an honor to be affirmed by you.

To the people in my space who have allowed me to talk through the harrowing experience that is life, thank you for your ears. Thank you for joining in with me to create spaces where we can share doubts, our sometimes faithlessness, and our gripes about the unfairness and indignities of life. In particular, I must give thanks to my brother Dennis who so graciously loaned me his ears, mind and time on certain evenings, as I traversed a PIT-iful season.

Finally, but certainly not least, to a group of unflinching, dedicated supporters who pre-ordered copies of this book – many of them in multiples – thank you for believing in me. It means more than you will ever know. Truth be told, had it not been for your pre-orders, I would have chickened out. On quite a few occasions, I contemplated returning the money, but it just didn't sit well with my spirit that I was writing about pursuing dreams, fulfilling assignments, and purpose and would not see this assignment to the end. So, thank you, thank you, thank you. I am grateful.

connect with me

I have, over the years, joyfully replied to thousands of emails from readers. It's the closest thing to the beauty and sacredness of letter writing; taking time to carefully organize one's thoughts and ideas without interruption, releasing them and allowing the recipient to respond without interruption. This is my preferred medium of communication. I say all this to say that I would love to hear from you, so take all liberty and shoot me an email at **hello@chadiamathurin.com** and I will respond. The email can be on your thoughts about dreamer., how it has impacted you, or something totally unrelated that you feel impressed to share with me. Looking forward to hearing from you.

Made in United States
Orlando, FL
15 January 2024

42513256R00082